SON

OF

A

PIONEER

AN AUTOBIOGRAPHY OF THE LESSONS OF LIFE AS TAUGHT FROM THE HOME HEARTH

LESSONS AND ANTIDOTES TAUGHT TO

PETER M. LEAMING

SON OF THAT PIONEER

DEDICATED TO MY DAD

ARTHUR L. LEAMING

FRIEND

PIONEER

HUSBAND

FATHER

TEACHER

PATRIOT

Prepared and written for:
Daughters: Gail and Laurie
Sons-in-law: William and John
Grandchildren:
Brent, Lance, Atura, Jaron and Brenna
They often ask me what it was like
"When I was a boy."

Pioneer defined.

Someone who is among those who is first to enter and settle a region, thus opening it up for occupation and development by others

Other Books and Articles by the Author

- o Col. Pete's Korner
- o *History of the Ellijay Seventh-day Adventist church from 1890-2012*
- o Life Poetically - Three Generations (Poems and Essays.)
- o *Will the Vatican rule the World and the Oath of the Jesuit Order*
- o Is the USA dying? (Six-part series.)
- o *Life on the thin Blue Line (My police officer's story.)*
- o America Today as I see it (Seventy-part series.)
- o *Son of a Pioneer (Autobiography.)*

The moving finger writes and having writ, moves on: Nor can all thy piety nor wit shall lure it back to cancel half a line, nor all thy tears wash out a word of it.
(Omar Khayyám 1048-1131),

CONTENTS

Introduction 13
Author's Note
Slang Phrases
How to Survive a Heart Attack Alone
From the Heart by Red Skelton
Life is a Battle 26
Lessons of Life From the Home and the Heart
Living in Drury, My First Home
Living in the Whare
We Move to Waiau Pa
Uncle Sandy & the Marois 41
Rabbits
Living with Aunt Marjorie
Aunt Edith
Uncle Stan
Together as a Family 47
0Three Little Pigs and the Big Bad Wilf
Arthur Fennell
Blind Calf, Rabbits & Red Beach
Scrub Lambs
Handcuff Bush, Pocket Knife & Kumera 50
Timber Cutting
The Cowshed
Farm Life & Cows
Pre-Electric & Post Electric
The Cream Separator 59
Hot Water
Condy's Crystals
Jam and Jars
Hunting & Pheasants
Frerery & Soeurey 65
Santa's Elves
My Saddle
The Dunny

Fruit, Veggies, & Flowers
Party Line   69
Angels
School
Reggie Carter's Orchard
Fight at King's Garage
Home Guard Unit   78
Birds and the Bees
Meat & Butter
Bicycle
Fishing for Whales
Long Pants   81
The Bull
Bringing in the Cows
Turnips, Swedes & Ice Cream
Water Tank
Going to Auckland   85
Fish & Chips & Hot Jam
Weekly Bath
Golden Syrup
Harvest Time
Tin Roof   88
Milking Time
Scottie
Miro Tree
The Five Sisters
Tea-Time   93
Two Horse Team
Hay Sweep
Things of the Sea
Native Bush – Trees and Flax
Weeds & Hard Work   99
Father's Forgiveness
Evenings Around the Fire
A Bible Word
Dad and Recent History   102

Name That Spot
Appendicitis
Joan's Swimming Hole
My First Suit and Shoes
Nikau, Kumeraho, Sulfur, Treacle & Boils 105
The Tax Snooper
Watch the Lions Feed
Jimmy O'Goblins
Sharp Tools, Strong men
What is a Fact?   109
Marriage & Money
A Penny Horrible
Hospital Motion
Another Cripple
Step-Mother First   112
Mick or Mack
The King & the Pope
Don't Waste a Grave
The Pick Handle
Dad and Poems   117
Approbation
Black as a Priest's Heart
Tabacco & Wine
What is Money?
Man, Mosquitoes, Calf   121
Harvest Food
Oatmeal & Water
New Zealand Scone Recipe
Harvest Beer
Kill and Butcher   126
Twelve Baskets Full
Robert Reece - Poem
Flying Breadknife
Smoke-O
Picnics in the Bush   132
Mother Earth
Learning Poems

Clearing the Land
Are We Faithful Trustees
Cute Saying   136
Was it Heavy Son?
Vot am I?
God Said to Moses
Kewpie Doll
The Moving Finger   139
Morse Code
Absolutely Useless
Monkey's Birthday
Bonswere
Fighting   142
A Country Job
Little Wooden God
Slashing Thistles
Jaw Harps
Bottom In, Bottom Out   147
Women
Spelling Words
Twenty Pound Note
Sympathy
Knowledge   150
Rolls C'nardly
Leaving the Nest
Leaving Home for Good
Gas and a Dentist
A **Dance at Waitoki**   152
Royal New Zealand Airforce
My Companion in the Airforce
Home from War
After World War II Was Over
Dad's Favorite Sayings   158
Jokes
Pubs
A Bun Fight
Edison's Phonograph

Dad & History   162
New Zealand Birds
New Zealand's Monetary system
Trees Native to New
Looking Back   170
When I Was a Boy
Now I Am a Grandfather
Photos   **176**
Postscript

AUTHORS INTRODUCTION

This book is written in fond memory of my Father,
Arthur Lawrence Leaming,
Our family, and the 156 acre farm in Wainui
Kaukapakapa,
New Zealand, and my growing up, 1927 and on.

The original acreage was deeded to the Fennell family
by the Crown (Queen Victoria) in the late 1800's.
Reginald Fennell, a son, of the original owner, sold
156 acres of land to my father in 1930. The original
owner had 3 children. Reginald, who sold the land to
my Dad, a daughter *(Carrie)* who married Henry
Lloyd, whose grandsons still own both the Fennell
and Lloyd properties, and Arthur, who never married.

The following is written in sequential order, as much
as possible, as the memories of come to mind.

Our address was
Wainui Rural Delivery, Kaukapakapa.
(Land of muddy water)
New Zealand

Kaukapakapa (Pronounced *Cow Copper Copper)* was
the rail head, Post Office, General Store, Butcher
Shop and the local Pub. The small township was
about 12 miles away. The general store and butcher
shop, a combination, was owned by the Dye family,
who made deliveries of various food items, meat,
bread etc. and the newspaper, the *"Herald"*, Mondays,
Wednesdays and Fridays by van. (*A V8 Ford Van).*

Personal service was really the watchword in those days. Alas, it is no more. We very seldom went to Kaukapakapa. Mr. Dye was very good to my Dad, letting him run up a food bill of about ninety pounds. This was a tremendous amount in those days. I well remember the day that Dad, who had just sold a load of posts, paid off the amount. Mr. Dye was so pleased he insisted Dad take a few sweets for me.

As a very young child my mother left us. My sister Delphine about 8 months old and I myself was barely three. At that time we lived in Drury, just south of Auckland. After we left Drury, our time was alternately spent at Waiau Pa with Uncle Harold's family, and on the new farm in Wainui, which Dad had recently purchased.

Uncle Harold and Aunt Dolly, his wife, had four children. Elsie, Muriel *(Bub)*, Thelma and Leslie, *(Dooley)* all older than my sister or myself. With the exception of my sister, we all had to work milking, cleaning up, feeding stock, etc. Uncle ran a dairy farm and later on added pig raising on a fairly large scale. Most dairy farmers raised a few hogs as there was plenty of skim milk left over after the milk separating process. This was an extra bonus, somewhat like frosting on a cake. The dairy farmer's paycheck came from the cream supplied to the local co-op, which made butter and cheese.

Uncle Harold's pig raising venture raised quite a few eyebrows. There was a slaughter house about a mile away and Uncle acquired the offal and all the parts not used, and boiled them down for the pigs to eat. Guess who had to help scrounge for the wood used in the cooking process? After a while there was a never ending stink in the air that had a nauseating effect on all in the immediate vicinity. People were given directions to Uncle's farm as follows. "Go to Kettle's general store at the intersection, take the beach road about 1/2 mile, and when you smell a horrible stink, that's the place." I have np doubt that if the wind was in the right direction, instructions would not have been needed.

Looking back some eighty years, I have concluded, that our way of life then was pretty good, somewhat primitive by today's standards, but still rather good. We were happy and carefree in spite of all the never ending work, seemed to find time for play and to have childhood adventures.

I don't remember exactly when my sister Delphine and I went to live on the farm in Wainui. It was after Dad built the 3 roomed home, probably1934, from lumber we sawed from timber on the farm. My aunt Nan came to keep house and look after us. I was often there at the farm with Dad prior to the house being built; my sister Delphine was left at Waiau Pa during these interludes. The three roomed house in Wainui was built with a bedroom on each end, the middle being the kitchen and living area.

Later this kitchen was turned into another bedroom when the other side of the house was built. This included a formal living room at the front *(hardly ever used and was a complete waste)*, family room and eating area *(with fireplace)* complete with a tiny kitchen in the middle, and laundry, bathroom etc. at the rear *(note, no inside toilet facilities)*. The toilet (one hole) was down the path about 20 feet from the back door. Toilet paper was not available, but the Sears Roebuck catalog was.

The laundry consisted of a hearth for a fire and a large copper boiler in which clothes were boiled, rung out by hand, rinsed out again and put on the outside clothes line to dry. The copper boiler was also used to steam the Christmas pudding every year.

Eventually we acquired a hand operated wringer, and after I left home a clothes washer. *(Primitive by today's standards.)* Really dirty clothes were first rubbed on the scrub board to loosen the grime. Our hand washing basin was perched under the taps *(faucets)* on a 12" piece of lumber cut to fit snugly across and about half-way up the bath tub. Our back door was never locked, although we did have a key for it.

My bedroom was at the rear of the house and was about 8' X 9', just enough room for two single beds and a small clothes dresser. There were no built in closets in any of the bedrooms.

What follows are some of my adventures and happenings as a young child; As an adolescent, and as a young teenager growing up.

AUTHOR'S NOTES

New Zealand, *(Aoteroroa - A-oh- tea a row ah)* Maori Name for the land of the long white cloud. The land "Down-under." New Zealand, until recently was a country not generally known by the world's population. New Zealand, the home of the Maori, the land of thermal activity, the land of millions of sheep, the land where fishermen go for the big ones, the land that once won the "America's Cup Yacht Race."

New Zealand, the land where Christmas is always in the Summer time, the land where the people are always laid back, the land where I was born and educated.

I remember the great depression and Dad going off to work with a road crew, the Model T Ford and Essex, automobiles, Vulcan and Diamond T trucks. , the Edison Phonograph and the round cylinder records, and the newfangled invention - the Radio and the promise of television soon to come.

I remember seeing my first airplane and my first ride in a Gypsy Moth, the first machine that milked cows and a machine that separated whole milk into cream and skim milk, our first electric light and the electric hot-water heaterI remember our family weekly bath whether we needed one or not, the 14 party telephone line we were on, World-war Two and how I managed to finally get into the service *(RNZAF)* Royal New Zealand Air Force and be sent to the South Pacific Theater a little while before Japan's surrender. When we heard that the American Air had Force dropped an "Atom Bomb," we all asked the same question, *"what the hell is an atom bomb?"*

And I remember life on the farm, the long hours, the hard work and the hard times in which we lived,
the blazing fireplace about which we all gathered in the evenings where we were taught the basics of the adult life to come.

"The lives of great men all remind us, that we can make our lives sublime. And departing leave behind us, Footprints on the sands of time". *(Henry Wadsworth Longfellow)* These simple words written for me by my teacher have influenced me greatly.

Love for one's fellow man is mentioned in various ways in the Bible over 600 times. Thus the inspired Bible writers portrayed throughout the scriptures, lessons for mankind that God knew were important and necessary for His children to learn and understand, and more importantly, put into daily practice.

Consider Romans 13:9 "Love your neighbor as yourself...."

1 Corinthians 13:2 "....Without love I am nothing...."

1 Corinthians 13:4-8, 13 "Love is patient, Love is kind, it does not envy, it does not boast, it is not proud. It is not rude, it is not self-seeking, it is not easily angered, it keeps no record of wrongs, Love does not delight in evil but rejoices with the truth.
It always protects, always trusts, always hopes, always perceives. LOVE NEVER FAILS...
The greatest of these is love..."

Psalms 118:2 "...His (God's) love endureth forever."
The articles, short-stories, dissertations, poems and comments included here, come from many different sources, and have been gleaned, or written by me over a long period.

They cover many different subjects, and were written as the Spirit moved, as they came my way or as I felt impressed to write at that particular time.

Some are true life stories, and come from personal experience, some from the internet, some from other people I have traveled with, and some from quotations or comments found while reading. Others have come from memory, heard long ago. Whatever, the source, I have tried to mention the author, if known.

Many, I have written myself. Quite possibly some of the enclosed articles have been printed elsewhere at one time or another. I have included some that have come my way over the years even if the origin is not known or remembered. I feel it would be a shame if they were to be lost.

I am especially thankful to my two daughters, Gail Jorgensen and Laurie Grant, for their encouragement and persistence in having me write my memoirs, and other stories so they may be passed onto our grandchildren.

It is a task I have really enjoyed. Perhaps it may be considered a fringe benefit of living a relatively long life. I sincerely hope, you the reader, will enjoy my efforts.

SLANG PHRASES

Perhaps it would be a good start to acquaint the reader with a few of the phrases and slang words used by the Kiwis. Some have come from the English, some from Australia, most are in house. Many are still in common use.

Me Shelia	My girl friend
Odbod	Someone who does not fit the norm
Grog or booze	Usually means beer
Eski	Bag for carrying cold stuff
The trouble & strife	My wife. An English term
One over the eight	The number of glasses of beer, eight, generally considered to make someone drunk
Mate	Not your wife but a close pal
Cobber	Much the same as mate
Skinflint	Someone tight with money
Tuckered out	Tired
The Lu	An English term for toilet. In Scotland its called a Wee Wee hoose.
She'll be right	Everything is OK.
Tucker	Food
Tucker bag	How food is carried
Jumbuck	Australian word for sheep
LSD	Money (From the olden days of ponds, shilling & pence.)
Off his nut	He is crazy
Jimmy O Goblin	Slang term for money
Cozzy	A bathing suit
Don't get your knickers in a twist	Stay cool and don't panic
Cherrio	Good-bye - see you later
Traffic cop	Not the same as a constable
Bluey	A red headed male
Carrots	A red headed female

Ding dong	A male named Bell
Batch	A small week end cabin, usually without amenities
Ute	A small pick-up truck.
Cow cocky	A farmer who milks cows
Metal	Road gravel
Schitso	Someone who is schizophrenic
Bonza	Something really nice
Cuppa	Cup of tea
Snarlers	Sausages
Dog.	Bologna or Baloney
Barbie	Bar-b-q grill
Moving like a scolded cat	He's in a hurry
Tropo	He's been touched by by the sun, or a bit crazy
Ding bat	He's a bit off the main track
Chin wag	People having a chat
Back door trots	Diarrhea
Scared the daylights Out of him	He's probably seen a Ghost
Cot Case	He's done in; completely tired out; needs sleep
His puku	His stomach
Gropey mocca	Usually work or outdoor clothes

HOW TO SURVIVE A HEART ATTACK WHEN YOU ARE ALONE.

- Without help, if your heart stops beating properly and you begin to feel faint, you have only about 10 seconds to act before losing consciousness.
- You can help yourself by coughing repeatedly and very vigorously.
- Take a deep breath before each cough.
- The cough must be deep and prolonged, as when producing sputum from deep inside the chest.
- The cough must be repeated about every 2 seconds without let up until help arrives or the heart is felt to be beating normally again.
- Deep breaths get oxygen into the lungs and coughing movements squeeze the heart and keep the blood circulating.
- The squeezing pressure on the heart also helps it regain normal rhythm.
- Doing this will enable heart attack victim to get to a hospital.

FROM THE HEART

by Red Skelton

I have started with the, "Right from the Heart" rendering of the "Pledge of Allegiance" As presented by the late Red Skelton.

Skelton's Remarks Speak for Themselves.
Red Skelton, an unapologetic patriot, recited "The Pledge of Allegiance" in his own inimitable style on his TV variety show
The Red Skelton Hour," on January 14th 1969...

- **"I** (Me, an individual, a committee of one)
- **Pledge**　　　(Dedicate all my worldly goods to give without self-pity
- **Allegiance**　　(My love and devotion)
- **To the Flag**　(Our standard, Old Glory, a symbol of freedom; wherever she waves, there is respect because your loyalty has given her a dignity that shouts freedom is everybody's job)
- **Of the United** (That means that we have all come together)
- **States** (Individual communities that have united into 48 great states. 48 individual communities with pride and dignity and purpose, all divided with imaginary boundaries, yet united to a common purpose, and that's love of country)
- **Of America and to the Republic** (A state in which sovereign power is invested in representatives chosen by the people to govern.

- And government is the people and it's from the people to the leaders, not from the leaders to the people)
- **For which it stands: One Nation, Under God,** (Meaning so blessed by God)
- **Indivisible** (Incapable of being divided)
- **With Liberty** (Meaning so blessed by God which is freedom and the right of power to live one's own life without threats or fear of some sort of retaliation)
- **And Justice** (The principle or quality of dealing fairly with others)
- **For All** (Which means it's as much your country as it is mine)

Since I was a small boy, two states have been added to our country and two words have been added to the Pledge of Allegiance - **"under God."**

Wouldn't it be a pity if someone said that it had to be eliminated from schools too?

(Red Skelton 7/18/13 – 7/18/1997)

LIFE IS A BATTLE

This short biography was written for Share Him
Global Missions, May 2005,
*(After returning from a mission trip to Belize
where I was the main speaker.)*

I was born in New Zealand in 1927 and was raised on
a dairy farm. Life was a constant battle for survival.
There was usually enough to eat, but wearing apparel
was another story. I had my first pair of shoes when I
was about ten years old. School was 3 miles away
and there were no busses. Imagine; we actually had
to walk to school. When I was about 8 my father
bought me a bicycle, but I had a lot of flat tires. Then
I had to walk.

Church was almost non-existent in those days. Very
occasionally a circuit preacher held a service in the
tiny church about a mile from our home.
Times were hard, cash money was scarce, but we
managed to survive.

When I was 17 and World War 2 in the Pacific was
winding down, my father allowed me to enlist in the
Royal New Zealand Air Force *(RNZAF)*. After basic
training I was posted to the Pacific Theater and
served on Espiritu-Santu, Guadalcanal and Los
Negros until hostilities ceased. On the way home, via
a Catalina flying boat, at a layover in Santu, I was
bumped for someone more senior than I. Shortly
after take-off that particular plane was lost, never to
be heard from again. It was presumed lost
somewhere over the ocean. We went home the next
day.

After a working sojourn throughout New Zealand and
Australia, working at whatever came along, I signed

on as a second cook and baker on a British merchant ship bound for the USA and the UK. Conditions were so bad that I finally jumped ship in New York City and after being picked up by the FBI, was allowed to volunteer for the US Army.

After basic training I served for a while as a drill Instructor. Then I was posted to Japan and then on to Korea, where I served 5 months on the frontlines with 19th Regimental Combat team as part of a 4.2 mortar company, a part of the 24th Division. My duties were an ammunition bearer and service as a forward observer. I was then reposted to Japan for the remainder of my tour of duty.

Upon returning to the US in 1953, and after my discharge I was granted citizenship because of my military service. After a stint on the Rochester Police Bureau where I was, amongst other things, bodyguard to many notables such as Presidents Richard Nixon, John F. Kennedy and his brother Bobby, Governor Nelson Rockefeller and others. I later resigned and went into construction work.

1972 we moved to Florida where I set up my own construction building business. I retired to North Georgia in 1987 where I now reside. My wife, Brenda, and I are active in the Seventh-day Adventist Church in Ellijay, Georgia. We have 2 daughters and five grandchildren. We are enjoying life to the fullest.

As I said in the beginning, life is a constant battle for survival. I have fought in two wars and am now fighting in the greatest War of all time, that of the Great Controversy between our Savior Jesus Christ, and His adversary the Devil.

Our Lord Jesus won His fight for us and as a result so shall we.

Remember - *"Pray often, pray quietly with reverence, and don't ask for more than you need."*

AGE

Age is a quality of mind,
if you have left your dream behind.
If hope is cold; if you no longer look ahead,
If your ambition's fires are dead,
Then you are old.

But, if from life you take the best,
And if in life you keep the best,
If love you hold, no matter how the years go by,
No matter how the birthdays fly.
You are not old.

nknown)

LESSONS OF LIFE FROM THE HOME
AND THE HEART

The reader should try to understand the times, customs, and the feelings of the people of the time period about which I write. *(The 1930s and 40s in New Zealand)* Bigotry was not dead and in many cases neither was racial discrimination or snobbery. Even to this day these venomous snakes raise their ugly racial non-discriminating heads.

In those days the New Zealand native, the brown Maori, was not always considered the white man's equal. I was fortunate in that I grew up with Maori neighbors who worked the land, and I played with their children, never ever thinking about color, custom or spiritual differences. We lived and accepted each other as equals, as children do, and let the world go by.

Because of the many lessons learned from my brown brothers I will always be thankful to them and to my understanding family and relatives who lived alongside and worked with them. In many respects they were like the American Indian, in that they knew how to live off the land and how to embrace Nature's resources. The time period written about here was the middle nineteen thirties and early nineteen forties.

My father was a simple man, a man of high integrity, an honest man who believed in his King, his country and his fellow man in that order. He seldom gave way to anger but when he did it was time to move on for a while. He was only 5' 6" high, weighed 200lbs and was as solid as a tree trunk. He was powerfully strong and I remember his amazing feats of strength with awe. The neighbors nicknamed him *"Stump"* - as in tree stump.

Dad was very active in our community and was on all sorts of committees. When it came time for electricity to become an integral part of our lives he was right out there working, and as a result of his efforts, made it happen.
The power company was running a line Northward from Auckland and was about to bypass our area. Dad visited all the neighbors, always walking sometimes many miles, and secured a written pledge from each as to the amount they would pay yearly, even if they didn't use that amount. As a result of all these signed pledge/petitions the power company routed extra lines to our area and our entire area/neighborhood had the benefit of electricity.

Up to this time the household lighting had been with kerosene lamps, mantle lamps and candles.

Many of the farmers used diesel engines to run their milking machines and continued to do so even after electricity came, as there were many power interruptions, sometimes for long periods. For many years afterwards diesel power was considered much more reliable.

My Dad was well liked and well respected in the community and was eventually made a Justice of the Peace *(JP)*. However, he would not sit in court for minor cases where he could judge. He told me that he would not, could not sit in judgment of his fellow man, and remarked that, "There but for the grace of God go I."

He ran for a seat in parliament on the Labor Party ticket several times but was always defeated by the incumbent.

Later, when a Labor party representative was elected for the area, he served for many years on the Labor Representation Committee eventually becoming the chairman. This particular committee advised the local representative in parliament as to what the constituents in the area were interested in and offered timely advice.

The committee members were somewhat like the American lobbyist, except when the committee spoke, the representative had better listen if he wanted to be re-elected.

When Dad died, I received many letters from members of parliament and one from New Zealand's Prime Minister, Sir Walter Nash. *(shown on the following page)*

HOUSE OF REPRESENTATIVES
WELLINGTOM, NEW ZEALAND

Telephone: Office 49 090 -
Extension 437

Sir Walter Nash., G.C.M.G., CH., MP

March 22, 1968

Mr. Peter Leaming
150 Wedgewood Park,
ROCHESTER,
New York.
<u>N. Y. 14616, U.S.A.</u>

Dear Mr. Leaming,

It was not until a short time ago that your aunt, Mrs. Woolsey, advised me as to the passing of your father, and I am sending this note to express my appreciation with personal knowledge of the great understanding work that your father did for the Labour movement in a most difficult area.

I knew him in the earlier years of his association with the Labour Party, and I was always greatly impressed by his self-sacrifice, his unassuming character, and his great integrity. I am sending this note because I wanted to pay tribute to one of the great men of our movement.

I hope things are going well with you, and if you come back to New Zealand I would like to meet you at any time.

Kind personal regards.

Yours Sincerely,

Walter Nash.

Dad was a man with a voice for the time during which he lived. He believed in the motto *"Do it right and do it well the first time."*

As we were growing, up many of the values and lessons were taught with the family all sitting around the fireplace, the family hearth, in the kitchen/living room. This fireplace was the only source of heat we had year-round, and so this area was the most popular room in the house, especially during the winter months.

Questions about many issues were asked, answered and explained. It was kind of being in a learning academy. Dad had travelled about quite a bit, and so had much more information than we did. The radio was a new invention and we only received newspapers three times a week. Due to the time between deliveries, the news was often late or out of date.

He was an avid reader of the *"Herald"*, the main newspaper from Auckland and of books from the local library.

And of course, the radio, that new invention, brought us other world news, and many thrilling serials and adventures. There were thrilling adventures such as *"The Lone Ranger"*, *"The Air Adventures of Jimmy Allen"*, *"Out of the Silence"*, *"The Green Hornet"*, and one Dad really hated; the American serial called *"Jane Ace."* He could not stand the horrible nasal voice of the program's star.

The radio was also Dad's link with government proceedings, as all debates and issues were aired via the radio. There was a government network, *(no advertising)* 1YA, (Auckland) 2YA, Wellington)

3YA, (Christchurch), and 4YA, (Dunedin). He listened very carefully, often commenting to step-mother when he felt things were not going the way he felt they should. The commercial network also had 4 main stations, 1ZB, 2ZB, 3ZB, 4ZB.

Sometimes, on special occasions a neighbor would come by for the evening, bringing a wind-up gramophone and some 78 rpm *(45rpm and 33 rpm records had not made an appearance yet)* classical or operatic records for our listening.

The various arias were discussed between record changing and wind-ups. As a result, my musical tastes have been somewhat that of a long hair over the years.

Growing up in New Zealand on the farm was an experience I will always treasure. While the work hours were long, *(everyone worked, children included)* we lived well and always had plenty to eat and a nice warm place to rest. Much of the food we ate came right from the land. We always had a big garden, an orchard for fruit, a garden for vegetables; eggs from the hens and meat from the animals we ran on the land. We usually killed once week.

As there was no refrigeration in those days, we often shared the animals we butchered with a neighbor. The abundance of all these natural foods early in life has, in my opinion, given me god health and longevity.

The local school was about three miles distant necessitating a hurried trip to be on time for classes. Late comers, the reason did not matter, were given several swipes of the large leather strap which our teacher used very readily for discipline purposes.

Today in American society he would be serving a lengthy tern in jail. However, we were not really abused, and the lessons and values he taught, have stood me in good stead throughout life.

We took a lunch to school usually consisting of two slices of bread with a meat dripping center flavored with pepper. *(Dripping was the meat drippings that fell into the pan while the meat was being roasted - mostly fat)* sometimes we had a large boiled potato and a small pinch of salt.

While I only went to the 10th grade *(American)* I have been admitted to college here in the US and have held up against those who have supposedly the benefit of a full 12 year education.

LIVING IN DRURY
The first home I remember. South of Auckland.

I barely remember living in Drury, but I remember wanting to go to school. I pretended, by being allowed to cross the lawn with my lunch in a strawberry box for a picnic. I can still visualize my father getting onto the public works truck *(called going on the dole)* to go and earn money so that we could eat.

Probably one of the reasons my mother left Dad and us were the rough conditions we lived under. My Mother had worked for the nobility in the U.K. before coming out to N. Z. as a domestic and found it hard to adjust to current conditions. When they had married Dad was working for the telephone company. Shortly after he had quit to follow his dream of being a dairy farmer. Mother apparently thought he had lost his mind, giving up a good secure job. She was not of the same pioneer caliber as Dad. Times were tough and housing was not all that it is today. Money was non-existent and some of the food we ate was given to us by kindly neighbors, or we tried to grow it. The ducks and chickens made gardening difficult, but we needed the eggs. The floor in our house in Drury had cracks in it and we could see the chickens running around under the house.

During this period, an incident happened that has remained with me all these years. I was playing outside behind the little barn. I stopped to urinate and was bitten on my pecker by a duck. Probably thought it was a worm. Ouch!! I can remember this incident, vividly, just like it was yesterday. Naturally a yell went up to high heaven and I had to have first aid and comfort. It wasn't funny.

In my opinion just because conditions were bad, there was no excuse for my mother leaving small children.

A marriage vow says for better or worse.

LIVING IN THE WHARE
(Wha-ree, Maori name for a house)

In Wainui, briefly when I was about 4 years old. The Whare, was built using Ponga fern tree trunks placed upright in the ground as walls; the chinks filled with paper and/or mud stuffed into the cracks. The roof was framed from long small tree trunks and covered with Nikau palm fronds platted to make the roof fairly waterproof. The fireplace was formed out of old galvanized tin. There was no door to the Whare, just an opening that faced away from the prevailing winds.

Bunk beds were formed out of small tree trunks dug into the earthen floor *(no flooring)* and sacking from cut down grain sacks, were tied across to act as the mattress. Straw was placed on the sacks. As a child I thought it was great.

Now I go out camping in conditions not much better and still enjoy it. This was how my father and his friend Theo Codlin lived for quite some time as they broke in the land getting it ready for cattle.

They both toiled from sunup to sundown. The lived very sparingly as there was very little cash available. Each Sunday for the week-end treat they took the shin bone of a cow, stripped the meat off, tied it with sting and boiled it. This was the weekly roast. Vegetables were added as they were plentiful and cheap.

The shin bone was also boiled, and thickener was added to the marrow, the result being a spread used for lunch sandwiches through the week.

Bread was also very cheap. To my mind this was pioneering. We were still living in the Whare when Dad caught a possum. He tied the back feet together and hung it on a tree. "Watch this" said Dad said to me as he tapped the possum lightly on the head with a stick. The possum instantly relaxed (*playing possum*). Next morning, to my surprise, there he was large as life sitting up on the tree limb looking at us. Dad then dispatched him. Good lesson for a 4 year old. My father taught me many valuable lessons, even at that early age.

Theo Codlin worked with and for my Dad while they were clearing the land. He was Dad's cobber *(friend)*, when I was very small. Dad told me in later years, that Theo once said to him that he would give anything to have one of those, pointing at me. He never married. When cutting the bush, if Theo found a tree with a bird nest in it, he would not cut it. *"I'll go back and cut the tree later after the birds have gone"*, he would say. Of course, he never did, and this man's memorials lived on after him for many years after he had moved on. Many years later, after I was fully grown, I bumped into Theo in a town called Waiuku and we had a beer together and reminisced about the early days often called the good ole days.

The bartender had a common pledge posted in writing above the bar that if anyone could drink a gallon of beer from the cup the bar had, the drinks were on the house for all who were there.

Theo sad, *"fill the cup."* He picked the cup up with both hands and glug glugged his way to the bottom, much to the delight of all who were there, including me. Quite a feat.

He later told me that when he had first seen the offer, he had gone to the pub across the street and drank a gallon of water to see if he could do it. He old this lie with a smile on his face.

WE MOVE TO WAIAU PA

Shortly after my parents parted, Dad took my sister and I to live with his brother Harold who lived in Waiau Pa. (*Pa was the Maori word for fortress, a place that could be easily defended*). Here we stayed while Dad was trying to buy a piece of land and resettle. Here at age 4 ½ I started school. One day I got a splinter in my finger. Miss Payne, the teacher took it out. There was no pain - I was a very surprised young man.

My uncle Harold had an old caterpillar tractor whose tracks had finally worn out. The men *(my Uncle Sandy and Dad)* wrapped the old worn-out tracks around the rear drive sprocket wheels and mounted an old Studebaker car's front end assembly and wheels on the front to steer with. The way the gearing was set up was indeed strange. To turn left the steering wheel was turned to the right and vice versa.

It always seemed odd to watch. However, this strange tractor helped plough a lot of fields. The engine was later brought up to the farm in Wainui, probably as a back-up engine for the sawmill. It now rests there in peace. If it hasn't been moved, I bet it I could still find it.

My uncle had a model T Ford.   One day as he and Aunt Dolly were going out, I, for whatever reason, held onto the spare tire, and as the car's speed increased I was afraid to let go (I was too scared to). My yells finally got their attention and the car stopped, but what a mess my poor bare feet were in, from running giant dragging strides on the gravel. Minor first aid was required.   To this day I don't know why I did such stupid thing.

The original Leaming *(prior to 1900)* farm in Waiau Pa backed up to the sea and had a large tidal flat that the family used for flat-fishing *(Flounder)* on the incoming tide.   The light we used to attract the fish was a carbide water lamp that was very efficient.   My great uncle used to spear flat-fish at night with a light a spear. I do not even remember his name, if I ever knew it.   His last name was Webb; he was my maternal grandmother's brother.

He was known as 'the swearer,'" or 'uncle swearer' to us young folk *(what a legacy to leave behind!)*.   I have never to this day, known a man with a fouler mouth than his. Every other word was a swear word or a profanity of the worst possible kind.   Even hardened menfolk would blanch at some of the the language he used.   It did not matter if there were ladies present, it was always the same.   At harvest time when the local farmer's wives fed the workers, the ladies would not allow him in their house.   He was fed him outside like the dirty dog he was. Good for them.   He was, however, a good fisherman.

UNCLE SANDY & THE MAORIS

My Uncle Sandy had a family of Maoris working for him who lived on his land out behind the barn. Old granny, as she was called, was into natural herbs and cures for her family and others. Once when my uncle Sandy had a really bad toothache, Granny said she could fix it. She went out gathering herbs and other things. She came back chewing some of them in her mouth. She took out a little round ball of whatever she had been chewing and asked my uncle to open his mouth and she placed the little chewed up ball of medicine *(masticated herbs)* onto his sore tooth and the pain was relieved. She never would tell us what the poultice consisted of. The Maori people possibly still have many secrets the have not shared with the Pakeha. *(The white man.)*

Maori Hangi - *(oven)*
This was/is the way Maoris' cooked for a feast in the olden days, and still do on some special occasions. I was privileged to attend several. A large pit was dug and rocks were placed in the bottom. A fire was then started to heat the rocks. Later, the fire was raked aside and wet mats were placed on top of the hot rocks and then doused with water. Food was placed on the mats and covered with more mats, more food, more mats, food etc. until the hole was full. The top covering mat was then covered with soil and tamped tight around the edge to allow the steam to rise up through the center. It took many hours for the food to cook but was well worth the wait.
A Maori party usually lasted several days.

RABBITS

In Waiau Pa the countryside was overrun with rabbits, as were a lot of other areas. They were descendants of the original few.
(14-brought to New Zealand by some stupid English noble or Lord for the express purpose of breeding them for sporting purposes.)

Now, there is no such thing as two rabbits!! Hence the saying, breeding like rabbits. The rabbits lived in colonies with burrows running every which way. There were quite a few of these colonies on my uncle's farm. The holes were a danger to livestock. The men folk set out to exterminate the population covering the holes with nets. Ferrets were then released into the holes and scare the bunnies out. It worked very well, but as I said there is no such thing as just two. Miss a pair and you are back to square one. Poisons worked, but again there was a limit to the kill. It wasn't until much later that the problem was solved because of its magnitude all over the country. A product called 'Myxomatosis' was injected into the males.

The infection then spread throughout the population killing almost all the pests. A few survived. Nature almost always takes care of a species. Later, Rabbit boards were formed in many areas, and trained men with dogs, poison traps and guns worked on the problem. The farmers were charged a nominal fee per acre owned. Some areas even erected rabbit proof fences. Other places made it illegal to hunt or shoot the pests, the reasoning being that people would usually eat what they shot.

All this because of seven brace *(pairs)* of rabbits.

LIVING WITH AUNT MARJORIE

As my sister and I were moved about, we were sent to live with the lady I called the butter-pat lady, my Aunt Marjorie, Dads youngest sister, and her husband Donald, who lived in Penrose, just south of Auckland. I was 7 years old. She was 20.

My aunt was called the butter-pat lady after I had helped churn butter on several occasions. The finished butter was patted into shapes with two wooden butter pats. These pats had lines running diagonally both ways across the pad. When the butter was shaped, little diamond shapes were left.

Aunt Marjorie kept me in line by telling me that if she spanked me with the butter-pat there would be shapes, like those on the butter, on my back-side. I believed her and behaved. In later years we had a good old laugh about my childhood gullibility.

Aunt Marjorie's husband, uncle Donald, played the violin and sang. He was some- what of a clown, especially after a few drinks, and would do a rendition of the classic song Danny Boy. The way he changed the words always gave us a good laugh.

When he came to the part, *"You'll kneel and say, instead of and art thou there for me,"* he would sing, *"My God doesn't he stink."* His violin playing opened a new world of musical instruments to me. Perhaps this is why I still thrill while listening to well played violin music. Thank you Uncle Donald A childish trick we used while in Penrose was to buy rock hard candy balls which sold three for a penny.

My sister Delphine and I devised a system to get four. We went to another store and asked for 2 halfpennies for the penny we had. Then we would go into the candy store and ask for a hapenth *(1/2d)* worth of the rock candy. The rock hard candy balls could not be split. We went in individually and each of us received two candy balls. Pretty neat eh! Looking back I am sure the store owner knew what we were up to but respected our ingenuity and went along with us. Who says children aren't smart.

Another episode was, going to the grocery store *(greengrocer's)* for a penneth *(1d)* of speckled fruit, fruit that had little rot spots. We pushed them out with our fingers before we ate. The greengrocer couldn't sell the fruit to his regular customers and we and other, children were able to enjoy good ripe fruit and help him recoup at least a penny or two. Eighty years later I still cut out the bad spots and eat. Perhaps, that is why I still love lots of fruit.

While we were staying with my aunt her first child Maria, *(now deceased)* was born. I had never seen a newborn child and remarked, much to my aunt's amusement that, that the baby looked like a wizened-up sausage.

Later when I was in aunt's bedroom, I noticed a picture of a man wearing a crown of thorns on His head. I asked who would do such a thing. My exact comment was. *"Why, is that silly fool wearing those thorns as a crown?"* The picture fascinated me then as it still does. I had never heard of anyone who would do something like that. My aunt, a converted Catholic, explained to me about Jesus and why He was wearing the crown. I was duly impressed and had my first contact with my Savior. Thank you Aunty.

AUNT EDITH

Several times during my younger years I visited *(I probably should say farmed out)* with my Dad's sister, Edith in Howick, about 15 miles out of Auckland. It was a very enjoyable experience. I was able to buy flavored ice blocks, about two inches square in a cone, made for the block, for a penny. Whenever I was sent to the store for something I was usually treated to one. An interesting note is that later my aunt moved and lived in the new place, at 11 Cockle Bay Rd, for over 50 years, and only left it when she became too old to care for it. She was born on the 29th November 1899, living into her nineties.

Another treat I enjoyed as a child was a small bag of sherbet and a jube *(a soft jelly like candy)* on a stick. The jube was licked and then dipped into the sherbet until it was gone, and then the jube was polished off. This treat also only cost a penny.

UNCLE STAN

When I was 10 years old I went by myself on a train (it took an entire day) to visit my uncle Stan on his farm in Edgecumbe in the Bay of Plenty. He had a nice riding horse which he allowed me to ride and I had a great time. One morning, while out riding, I noticed smoke coming from a haystack. *(It was hay making season)* I rode back to inform Uncle Stan. We rode out together and found that the haystack was on fire internally.

He pulled the top off the stack and cut a hole in the center with an ensilage knife to try and put the fire out. It was hot work and after a while he came out of the hole and down to the ground for a break. Just as he reached the ground a sheet of flame erupted out of the hole where he had been working and shot upward about 10 feet. Had Uncle been in the hole he would have been fried.

Uncle Stan said a bad word or two or three, reached into his pocket and for his cigarette lighter, and walked around the stack lighting it as he went. I was there for two more weeks and the stack was still burning when I left.

Also, while visiting Uncle Stan, I experienced my first earthquake while we were out in the harvest field. Several years later, while visiting my uncle Don, who now lived in the same geographic area, I experienced several sharp quakes. They were and are common in that area *(Bay of Plenty)*. In later years while living in the city of Wellington, I experienced several more sharp quakes. In most cases only dishes rattled and furniture danced. In one instance it knocked people off their feet. Very, very scary; I felt so helpless, but there was nothing I could do.

Coming back by train to Auckland, Walker Brunton who was to meet me was a bit late. A man accosted me and invited me into a vacant car to wait. He got fresh and I left. When Walker arrived several minutes later I told him what had happened. He almost exploded with rage and stormed about looking for the man who by now had disappeared. Fortunately for that man Walker did not find him, a pity he didn't.

TOGETHER AS A FAMILY

And so, after all my travels I was back living in Wainui *(Why-nu-ee)* in the new house Dad had built. On and off, I had been there part of the time, now it was for keeps, we were finally all together as a family. Dad had also built a small cowshed, barn and pigsty. We were finally a family of farmers.

When I was allowed to go and play with the Ryan twins *(boys)* we would take round galvanized tin washtubs and put them in the creek as boats and play navies. The idea was to bump into the other ship and try to sink it. Lots of fun without expensive toys - also could be a little wet if you got sunk.
I will never forget the hot day when my sister Delphine, my stepsister Thelma and Alicia Ryan *(now a nun),* all danced naked on the bank while we boys were in our boats in midstream. They put on quite a show and it was very naughty if you remember that it was over 80 years ago. We never did tell on them either.
Perhaps we were hoping for a repeat performance, which incidentally never occurred, no matter how much we boys pleaded.

THREE LITTLE PIGS AND THE BIG BAD WILF

In the late 1930's one of our neighbors was a man named Clem Driffill. Now Clem was the dad of three pretty young daughters *(and a son).* There was Elva, Ethel and Ida and the swains quickly came calling on the girls.

As a young lad I would go up and visit *(someone said we are never too young)* and sometimes we would sit in the sun and chat. Elva's swain was called Wilfred.

Walker Brunton *(Dad's cobber)* also made calls. One day when he saw Wilfred going to visit, he said. "There goes the big bad 'Wilf' to visit the three little pigs." Elva eventually married Wilfred.

Ethel Driffill was a real lady, a wife, a mother, and a lifelong friend. Enter Selwyn Lloyd, our across the road, neighbor started courting Ethel, one of Clem's pretty daughters. I can see her now on the back of his Panther *(one cylinder)* motorcycle, yelling hello to us as they sped past the cowshed in a swirl of dust. After they both had a nasty spill, he sold the motorcycle and bought a car. Soon afterwards they were married and lived happily ever after. Their two sons still live on *(as far as I know)* and run the family farm.

Ethel and I stayed in touch over the years, and she did Brenda and myself the great honor of the being honoree grandmother at my daughter Laurie's wedding in Ft. Pierce, Florida. *(my real mother would not come).* Ethel travelled all the way from New Zealand for the event. She carried a real home-made New Zealand wedding cake, complete with almond frosting underneath a hard frosting on top.
When coming through customs she was asked what was in the box

"A real honest to goodness New Zealand wedding cake complete with all the almond frosting and icing," was her tart reply. *"If you want to open it, alright, but if you do, you will darn well pack it up again."*

They never opened it. They passed her through. The cake of course was a real hit with everyone present. This lady who carried so herself regally, and acted like a queen, was a good sport and her unique laughter very contagious. She passed away at age 81 and will be sorely missed.

ARTHUR FENNELL

Another of my Dad's cobblers *(son of the original owner of our land)* was a man named Arthur Fennell who had traveled extensively and had worked and walked his way across the U.S.A. in the 1920ies. He was a most interesting, very soft spoken, unassuming man. He knew how to work and work hard.

As a boy I was in compete awe of him because of his travels and the stories he would tell. He and Dad were of the same political persuasion *(labor)* and many a discussion revolved around the country's problems. He died some years after Dad, when he was in his mid-nineties, and died on the job, still working. A really nice soft-spoken gentleman.

BLIND CALF, RABBITS & RED BEACH

When the bull was a calf and we realized he was blind Dad did not have the heart to destroy him. We watched him grow and he seemed to prosper and know where to get the good grass and the water. As he grew he followed the cows around and seemed to know where the good feed was. Perhaps his hearing was more acute. He was sleek and fat.

When Dad shot him to butcher for food, he staggered and fell into a shallow well and we had a difficult time getting him out. Dad corned the meat *(no refrigeration in those days)* and the method he used was to put enough regular salt into a cut down barrel of water so that a potato would float. The meat was then immersed to cure. I ate so much corned beef that year that it was a long, long time before I really cared for corned beef. Now it is one of my favorites.

In Wainui the rabbit problem, earlier mentioned, was as bad. Again, it was finally solved by the use of a rabbit board years after I left home. The rabbit board finally bought the rabbit problem under control, *(the rabbit board still operates)* I have seen what looked like a whole hillside move at just about dusk.

From our home in Wainui to Red Beach was about 12 miles. We went on quite a few occasions whenever we could find a way, and always had lots of fun. Uncle Jim owned an old Essex sedan that he finally got running. We went to the beach one day and on the way home while going down a hill the brakes burned up. We were able to get home. After that escapade he sold the auto. *(I was about 8 years old).* In those days at Red Beach there were a few weekend shacks and a few permanent homes. Today it is wall to wall houses.

HANDCUFF BUSH, POCKET KNIFE & KUMERA

Handcuffing myself to a tree. I was playing I was a cowboy chasing the bad guys. Dad had purchased a toy gun, holster and handcuffs for me. Store bought toys of any kid were a real treat as I usually had to make my own.

The bad guys *(imagined)* got the drop on me and handcuffed my hands behind me to a three inch tree. Then the make believe became really serious; the toy handcuffs stuck, and I could not open them. I couldn't get free. I was probably there for several hours and was getting really scared as the day drew on. After yelling for a long time, Dad who had been working over in the bush nearby, heard me shouting and came to the rescue. To soothe my nerves he actually gave me a few puffs on his cigarette. That little strip of bush was called Handcuff bush from then on.

Dad gave me a lovely new pocketknife for my ninth birthday. I lost it the first day, causing me much grief. I surmised it had fallen out of my pocket through a hole. It must have caused Dad to be most unhappy too.

The Kumera was a Maori sweet potato, which we grew. A staple of the Maori diet and a part of their ancient culture. I never did like them. I still don't like sweet potato.

TIMBER CUTTING

Cutting timber on the back ridge. We called it Kauri ridge because of the multiple Kauri trees that grew there. The trees were felled and the end snipped, *(the edges cut at a 45 degree angle)* the bark peeled off, and using a timber jack to get them going, were sent to the swamp-bog at the base of the ridge. They snapped off smaller trees like matchwood, as they went hurtling down the hill. To get the logs out of the bog, Dad made a Wim. A round part of a large tree trunk, placed on end, with a long pole stuck into it to which a horse *(which Dad rode home, 30 miles at a walk, for fear he might drop dead)* was harnessed and walked around and around. My job was to keep the horse moving.

A long cable was attached to the Wim's body and as it wound onto the drum, the log on the other end on the cable was slowly pulled out of the bog, out onto the flat so that the bullock team could get to it. Crude but very effective. A make do with whatever you have situation.

After all the logs were out on dry land Dad hired Bullocky Blair and his team of twelve bullocks to pull them from the back flat to a place where trucks could get to them. Trucks, Diamond T models, pre-World war 2 were not very powerful or well geared and could not make the steep grade out from the flat.

I will never forget the names of the two lead bullocks, Sailor and Ginger. *(There were 12 total in the team)* The team owner was known as Bullocky Blair. He could swat a fly with his 12 foot whip which was attached to a long flexible wooden handle. It took both hands to wield it, and he was an expert - just ask the bullocks he had!

At night the bullocks had bells tied around their necks to make them easier to find each morning. Sailor and Ginger both knew how to put their heads on a bush or bushy tree shrub to prevent the bell from clanging. My job was to cover the area, find them and herd them in for work.

Who says animals are dumb? However once found, they accepted the fact, and were easily brought in.

The motorized Winch. On another part of the farm the timber had to be pulled out of the bush with a winch. It was anchored to the ground by a cable attached to large log. The log was buried long-ways in a deep ditch. I don't know who owned the winch but it sure was a marvel. It was moved by tying the cable to something immovable and letting it haul itself along on skids, or moved with a team of horses.

I must have been at school when it arrived as it was there one day when I arrived home. It had a gasoline engine with a 55 gallon drum of water as a cooling system. Very cumbersome, but quite effective. We used it to get the timber out from the central part of the farm.

Uncle Jim operated the winch controls while he watched me for signals. I was some distance away so that I could hear my Dad's commands as he guided the logs out through the trees with a timber jack. Some commands I recall were - *"Let go"*, *"Stop"*, *"Go very slowly"*, *"Haul away"* Each command could be heard by me, and was signaled to Uncle Jim, who due to the noise of the engine could not hear them. I felt very grown up that my Dad, who had impressed me as to my usefulness, trusted me literally with his safety. So nice to be trusted.

Not all the timber we harvested was sold. Some was milled and used for the house, barn and cowshed. The home-built sawmill was powered by an old Vulcan truck engine that seemed to use more gasoline than an airplane *(gasoline was still cheap then)*. The Vulcan truck was old, pre-war, and had been used by a neighbor to haul firewood. The tires were solid rubber and made for a bumpy ride.

Mounted on a frame for the mill the engine was cooled with a 55-gallon drum of water, which would boil when we had been milling for a while.

 My job was to open the throttle as Dad breasted the log into the spinning saw blade. The log, sat with one end on the saw bench, and the other end rested on a little 4 wheeled trolley mounted on wooden rails. The log was bulled *(pushed manually)* into the spinning blade and manually pushed and pulled through. Uncle Jim tailed out. He had a little trolley at his end also. I shut the throttle off as soon as the log was almost through. As I shut off the throttle a sheet of flame would shoot out about a foot long. The first time it did it scared me. Uncle Jim then sent the flitches *(pieces)* back for another cut until the lumber was milled to size.

The lumber was crude and rough but did the job. There was no automation and only rough gauges. Brute strength hept the logs straight. There were rollers on the bench and the saw blade was kept cool by having two tiny jets of water sprayed onto it *(one on each side)* underneath the main bench. My other job was to move the sawdust away while the men were getting the next log ready which had been hauled into place by a horse.

Cant-hooks were used to roll the logs up onto the bench and trolley. The sawdust pile was visible next to the cowshed for many years afterwards. Looking back, it was primitive but effective. Our house was built using this lumber and is still lived in some 80 years later. In contrast to the way the youth of today feel and act, I never felt put upon when called on to work. Actually, I felt honored that I was able to help my father.

THE COWSHED

In the early days before we had a covered cowshed, Dad milked the few cows we had *(outside)* by hand. He then walked about 6 miles to a rock quarry.
He had to be there by 8am. He would swing a 12 pound mall all day, breaking up rocks so they could be fed into the rock crusher. Then he had to walk the 6 miles home to milk the cows before going to bed.
I usually had the cows in and had started the milking before he arrived home. In the mornings he would leave early and I finished the washing chores. Times were hard and he could not even afford a bicycle.

When the owner of the quarry *(Sam King)* blew the starting whistle at 7.55am, the noon break whistle at 12.55pm and the knock off whistle at 5.05pm my Dad, and his friend Arthur Fennell, booked in an extra 15 minutes of time and were promptly fired on the spot.

The quarry owner was later killed. He was run over by one of his own trucks driven by his son and not many, if any, of the locals mourned him.

Dad had milked the cows by hand outside regardless of weather. In New Zealand the rainfall averages about 50 inches yearly. As you may guess the odds were 50-50 it would be raining. I can see Dad now leaning against the cows in the pouring rain so that the water running off the cow's side would not go into the milking bucket. After several years he built a cowshed from the lumber we milled, roofed it with old iron that he scrounged from somewhere. The roof had to be patched often with rags and tar to keep us dry. It lasted about 20 years. When we finally got electricity, Dad bought a Gaines milking machine and a separator motor. Electricity had just recently arrived. Many neighbors used Lister diesel engines to power their milking machines, prior to the electricity coming, and for a time afterward, as many did not trust this new invention called electricity which at best was unreliable for some time. Many times, when the electricity was off, we had to continue milking by hand.

This cowshed lasted for over 20 years and it was here, as I grew up, and my father taught me many things that have lasted a lifetime. I shoveled my fair share of cow manure, (*we had another name for it*) washed my fair share of cow's tits, scrubbed my fair share of milking machine parts and waded through more than my fair share of sometimes knee deep mud. I fed my fair share of calves, pigs, hens and cows too.

It was here, in the cowshed, that I learned the Morse code which Dad had written on the wall with charcoal. I learned the way telephone lines were strung in a clockwise pattern to avoid electrical interference, life's values, moral values, family cohesiveness and loyalties, what is expected of a man, and all the things that a young man should know.

FARM LIFE AND COWS

I was instructed about the native timbers and flora, etc. I also learned about cattle breeding and how to know when certain cows would be calving. *(Just watch the bull, and then count forward to calving time)*

The work was hard, the hours were long, but the lessons learned have sustained me for a lifetime. Dad sometimes reinforced his lessons with a slap or a spanking, but never in anger. He was a wise, honorable, loving, gentle man.

Whenever a cow had a bad quarter *(cows have 4 tits)* we would identify the quarter from the position of the cow in the stall. That is, if we were facing the cow's udder, the front tit furthest away was top out, and the back one was bottom out and so on. Since most of the cows had their favorite stall and usually came into the same one each milking, it was easy to know and treat a bad quarter medicinally.

All the animals, the cows, the bull, the pigs, the dog, and the horses had names. Mostly the cows had female names, but sometimes the name was given to fit the cow, much like the American Indian's custom. That is, long tits, gimpy, one horn, short tail etc.

Animals on a farm are distinctive and easy to recognize, just like people. While the bull usually had a name he was mostly referred to as 'The Bull.' In many cases that was a lot of bull as many were quite large.

Our two horses were Sandy and Tommy *(both geldings)* and were allowed to finish out their days just doing nothing after we acquired a tractor.

Dad felt that they had earned their retirement. The dogs *(over the years we had several)* knew and answered to their names.

In spring when the grass was lush and plentiful, the cows would gorge, especially on clover. They had to be watched closely for instances of 'Bloat.' *(Gas build up causing the cow's stomachs to swell up to a dangerous level.)* Not too many people realize that cows have four separate stomachs. Not treated, a cow would die. To release the gas a drench, *(A cow's Alka-Seltzer or Bromo-Seltzer)* would be poured down their throat.

On rare occasions if this did not work, a knife would be inserted back near the cow's hip to let the gas out. This was a dangerous practice and only very rarely used, and then only to try and save the cow's life. Either way, if the cow belched, or the knife was used the smell was awful.

Danger - never stand behind a cow in spring-time. The lush spring grass also made the cow's stool very, very loose. If you were standing behind a particular cow and she coughed as she was defecating, the resultant stream of waste could travel 10 to 12 feet. Pity the poor person caught in the wrong place. We all learned the hard way. Also, pity the poor dog who was often sprayed and then needed to be bathed, a chore which did not make him too happy. Not that he hated water. Often, in hot weather, he would cool down by jumping into the creek and splash around.

PRE-ELECTRIC & POST ELECTRIC

Prior to the advent of electric power, meals were cooked on a wood stove. The sources of interior illumination were candles and the mantle lamp. For reading, which everyone did a lot of, I often thought that the mantle lamp gave better light than the electric. But the mantle lamp required being filled with fuel, and care had to be taken not to bump the lamp for fear of breaking the delicate mantle. Even a tiny knock or bump would break the mantle. Remember, there was no TV. TV only became realty in the very late 1940's, and even then wasn't that great. It was a new novelty however, something we looked forward to.

Electric lights however, were simply a flick of a switch and was much easier. At the cowshed it made a world of difference as the milking could now be done by machine. Electricity also made the separating and pumping of the skim milk to the pig pens easier. An electric hot water heater made wash-ups a cinch.

THE CREAM SEPARATOR

In order to get money for necessities, all the milk had to be separated into cream and skim milk. The cream was picked up every day and taken to the factory by truck to Helensville, to The Kaipara Dairy Co-op to be made into butter. The skim milk was saved for our pigs.

The separator was mounted on a solid table and, and before electricity, had to be operated manually *(my job)* by turning a geared handle. When the proper speed was reached the bell, which would ding with every handle turn, would then start to click. As long as the bell was only clicking the milk would be properly separated into cream and skim.

Just try to imagine what it was like turning that handle for about thirty minutes to get the job done *(my job of course).* Later, when the electricity came, we had a small clutch drive and motor to do the job. We kept the handle however, as sometimes the power would not be on.

All the skim milk, after we had electricity, was pumped over to the pig pens and stored in 55-gallon drums, which stood out in the sun. The skim milk curdled and turned into potent joy juice. The pigs loved it and got fat on it. So did the hens and the seagulls. *(we were only about 7 - 8 miles from saltwater as the crow flew)*

Have you ever seen see a drunken pig, or a drunken hen? You would die laughing. As far as the seagulls were concerned there was hardly ever a tern un-stoned.

HOT WATER

Before electricity, and for several years afterwards until we could afford an electric hot water heater, we heated water with a Califont. It consisted of an outer jacket and an inner jacket with water in between. A fire was built in the center *(my job was to get the wood and kindling)* with the larger fuel placed at the bottom and the kindling at the top. A funnel directed the air down to the fire *(there was a separate chimney)* and heated the approximately 10 gallons of water to boiling in a few minutes. Cold water went in the bottom and came out the top. If a good fire was kept going the water would continue to come out hot for as long as needed.

Hot water was needed to clean and wash all the milking equipment etc. Sometimes we even took a quick shower consisting of a bucket of warm water poured over the body, soap up, and another bucket of warm water to rinse off. The Califont was a really good water heater. These same heaters were also used in the cities with a gas fire box. Later on we acquired the electric water heater.

(Note - *I recently called New Zealand to see if Califonts were still available. I was informed the only way to find one was to visit the Museum. So sad*)

CONDY'S CRYSTALS

Condy's Crystals; Permanganate of Potash. They were/are about the size of Epsom salts crystals and are a bright violet in color. Mixed with water, the fluid was used as a disinfectant; just add a pinch to a 2 gallon bucket of warm or hot water and the solution was ready to use. We used the solution when helping cows to calve or pigs to farrow. Sometimes, when a cow was having trouble calving, Dad's whole arm length had to be inserted and used to turn the calf or to assist with the birth. His arm, hands, and any instruments we used were always thoroughly washed with the Condi's solution before use. Great stuff. It is still available.

JAM & JARS

Making Jars and Jam. It has often been said that necessity is the mother of invention. We had no jam jars, or money to buy any, and wanted to make jam. So, we made our own this way.
Ingredients to make jam jars; some empty one-quart beer bottles, *(plenty of those on the roadsides - times haven't changed)* a bucket of cold water, a fire, and a thick branding wire ring that would sit on the lowest part of the bottle necks.

Method; heat the wire ring until it is red hot, place it

on the bottle neck to heat the glass until the glass was really hot, then dip the heated neck into the cold water and then tap the neck gently. Voila, a jam jar.

Admittedly the top was a bit rough and we had to be careful, but when washed out, they served the purpose. The finished jam was then put inside the bottle and many layers of white paper were placed over the hot jam and the sides were sealed with home-made flour and water paste. Skim off the top one-half inch of jam before eating.

One year the jam in these home-made jars did not set up at all. It was runny but tasted fine. Dilemma, what to do with it. Solution, whenever we had porridge for breakfast we used sugar and milk. Since no one else wanted the runny jam I was allowed to pour it onto my porridge in place of the sugar.
It tasted great and it lasted a long-long time. Waste not - want not. Today it would surely go to my waist!!

Because of economics were not allowed to have butter and jam together on our bread. It was either or. However, sometimes we managed to get past the watchful eye of our parents.

HUNTING RABBITS & PHEASANTS

I made my own shotgun shells. I used wax match heads in the striker instead of Fulminate of Mercury, blasting powder instead of gunpowder, and bits of junk as projectiles. Reflecting on it, and the materials used, it is a wonder I ever survived, and never blew myself up. However, the shells worked *(although they occasionally would hang- fire)* and were somewhat effective. I shot a lot of rabbits with homemade shells. The only black rabbit I ever shot,

I cured the skin and kept it for years. I never saw another.

Curing rabbit skins was accomplished using a bent piece of #8 fencing wire as a hanger for drying. The rabbit skin was as a whole piece, not cut down the middle. After the skins were cured and dried, there was always a ready market. They were sold to the furriers in Auckland for ladies fur coats *(perhaps even as mink)* etc. Anyway, they generated some much needed extra pocket cash.

Rabbit stew, poor man's chicken. Whenever I managed to shoot a rabbit we had rabbit stew and onions, or rabbit, pan fried in flour, as the main course. It tastes a lot like chicken.

The only pheasant I ever shot, was by sportsman's standards not correct, it didn't really count, in that I shot it while it was still on the ground. I was so excited that I began shouting for all the world to hear. One the men working for Dad suggested that I had better be quiet as it wasn't pheasant hunting season. I was thoroughly crestfallen but obeyed.

True to really stupid English tradition, Dad hung the pheasant for several days before cooking it. I have always thought this traditional method of preparing game to make it taste better and more tender, was stupid and unsanitary. I have heard that after being hung for several days and then cooked, only a few slices of the meat could, or should, be eaten at one time. Probably true, as the meat by this time was half rotten before being cooked. This may be why gout was so prevalent, in the UK in days of yore, amongst those who ate this kind of meat, and washed it down with lots of wine. Still tradition abounds even to this day.

My stepmother's traditional way of preparing steak was in deep hot fat. Rump steak was purchased, cut into one inch slices and cooked. She was a truly a wonderful cook. Her apple pies were made in heaven. Her fruit cake, scones, *(biscuits)* baked jam rolls etc. were comparable with the best. Garden fresh salads with her great salad dressing, will long be remembered by me. Her secret went with her to the grave. She also served her salads with cold roast beef which truly titillated the taste senses.

Lamb chops, lambs fry *(liver)* and bacon, especially for breakfast, was a treat I looked forward to with eagerness. As I said earlier - cooking was her one redeeming feature in my opinion. We ate well, and deserved to, considering the amount of work we did. Children today don't know what work is, and that is sad. Regretfully, a sign of the changing times.
I know, and am eternally grateful, that I have been able to instill good work habits into my two children.

Beef Sausages. *(Commonly called Snarlers)* Cooked with onions and gravy, fried by themselves, or curried. Sausages were eaten often as they were a cheap meal, tasted good, and were liked by all. They were made from beef scraps, bread and seasonings. Great cold for camping trips and walkabouts too. Note. A walkabout is an Australian term for a period of wandering about, not looking for anything in particular, but observing with interest, your surroundings.

Baloney - commonly called Dog. Since it was cheap, we ate a lot of it in sandwiches.

FRERERY & SOEUREY

MY DEAR, AND ONLY BLOOD SISTER
DELPHINE MARCIA LEAMING.
11/13/29 - 8/8/1960

We were great pals growing up and did many things together. We felt a common bond when Dad re-married and our stepmother favored her own two daughters. Delphine felt badly left out of the girl talk and activities. My stepmother barely tolerated me *(the feelings were mutual),* but she had to at least feed me and keep clothes on my back. In fairness, however, she was a good mate for my Dad and was good worker. Her big redeeming feature, in my opinion as a growing young boy, was that she was a great cook and kept a great table.

Delphine and I were buddies, blood buddies. When I was taking French at school, and she found out the words for brother and sister, *(Frere and Soeur)* she called me "Frerery", and I called her "Soeurey" from then on. On other occasions we spoke in op-gibberish, to the consternation of those around us who were unable to follow the conversation. We always had a good laugh about it.

I remember one time when Delphine had been naughty, Dad told her to go and fetch a suitable stick so he could discipline her. She was gone for quite a while. Eventually she came back dragging a small tree about four inches in diameter. "Here you are Dad, hit me with this," she said.Dad was incredulous for a moment and then he started to laugh. He gave her a big hug instead of the spanking.

What a great parent Dad was.

I often visited with Delphine after she married the first time to a man called Griffiths. He was a bastard of the first water, and I was glad when she got rid of him. She eventually married a nice man named Allen O'Sullivan and they adopted a boy they called Kerry Michael. She collapsed one evening and was rushed to the hospital where she died. We later found out that the doctor at the hospital had treated her for a heart attack instead of low sugar.

She was such a nice person, and a real genuine one. I still miss her and all her advice and laughter.

SANTA'S ELVES &
AN UNEXPECTED CHRISTMAS PRESENT

One Christmas, Delphine and I decided to let Dad sleep in. We secretly got up about 2.30 am and stole out of the house, got the cows in and milked them, washed up and were home and back in bed when Dad came in to wake me about 4.30am. He had slept a bit late.
"Time to get boy," he said. I didn't move. He called me again. I still didn't move. He started to get a bit angry. He called me again.

"I don't think I will get up this morning Dad," I said. *"Let's all sleep late."* When I thought he would really lower the boom I told him. Delphine came into my room and we told him and wished our Dad a merry Christmas. The look on his face said it all. He went back to bed and back to sleep. Of course we had to milk the herd a little earlier that afternoon to play catch-up.

MY SADDLE

One afternoon when I was out riding looking for a

newly calved cow. I was riding through shoulder high scrub, when the saddle cinch broke. The horse continued on leaving me and the saddle slowly settling to the ground. The horse, free of his burden, left me and headed for home and I had to carry the saddle all the way back to the barn. A long way for a little chap, as we were at the back end of the farm.

THE DUNNY

The Dunny *(lavatory or toilet)* was outside down the path, about 20 feet from the back door. This place was O.K. in fine weather, or in the daytime, but in bad weather, or at night it was a real scary adventure for young people and those who were timid. The wind whistled through the cracks in the walls and so did the rain if it was raining. There were mean looking wasps looking for the human honey, droning mason bees looking for a place to nest and various kinds of scary spiders and creepy-crawlers, who called the Dunny home. And probably rats and mice; truly a really scary place for the uninitiated and children with vivid imaginations, which we all had. I never really sat in state like some did. I did what I went for and left quickly.

Toilet Paper. When I was growing up there was no such thing as toilet paper, at least not for us. I had heard about it of course, but I never saw any of the rolled stuff until I left home. The first time I saw rolled toilet paper and saw the serrations on the roll, I thought that the pieces were a bit too small, so I risked it and used several pieces hoping no one would know.

I often smile now when I remember this. Perhaps I thought that people kept track of it by inventory.

Fashion Magazines & Newspaper. *(Poor man's TP)* The Dunny toilet paper was usually an old catalog or news- paper, anything that would serve the purpose for which it was needed. When out in the bush, or away from home, leaves and or grass sufficed.

The foot washing *(water changes for each foot)* kind of toilet was not installed in the house until many years after I had left home. The Dunny was a seat over *(a one-holer)* over a 10 gallon can with a handle, which had to be emptied every week. The contents sure did make the garden vegetables grow where it was emptied. The job of emptying the can was not one of my favorite chores.

Running shoes and a Sears catalog. It was a standing joke at our house that if anyone got diarrhea *(back door trots)* we would advise them to have their running shoes on and have the catalog handy so as to expedite the expedition.

FRUIT, VEGGIES, & FLOWERS

In our fruit orchard we grew apples, peaches, plums and other fruit. I was constantly in trouble for picking and eating the fruit before it was fully ripe. Vine-fruit was called Chinese Gooseberries. Now they are called Kiwi fruit because the American people tend not to buy anything with the name Chinese in it.

Passion fruit, and Tree tomatoes. *(Now called Tamarillos.)* Cape Gooseberries mostly grew wild. The Passion fruit vines were planted on a slight downgrade and a trench was dug to allow us to empty the Dunny contents there once in a while. The downgrade allowed moisture to spread out and the solids were buried by digging a new trench and covering the old. The vines literally sprang out of the ground and bore an abundance of fruit.

Our vegetable garden grew almost all of our food. As a child I hated spinach, and parsnips, I still don't like cooked carrots, parsnips raw or cooked marrow's *(sort of a messy squash - yuck!),* and pumpkin which was/is a vegetable cooked with meat in NZ.

I liked Swedes *(rutabagas)* cooked or raw, potatoes, raw turnips, tomatoes, peas, beans, potatoes, beetroot, *(beets)* cabbage, cauliflower, and all kids of salads, etc.

Stepmother loved flowers. Her garden was truly a work of art. At the local women's group meetings she nearly always got a top prize. Her secret was Dad. He collected dried cow pies in a bag which she would chop up and dig into the soil. Dad did a lot of the digging also. The original Honey-do man. One day while Dad was cleaning up and burning the rubbish the fire got away from him and Dad and scorched the prize roses. He raced back to the house, got a bucket of water, and quickly doused the blaze. Stepmother was upset but finally forgave him.

PARTY LINE

Our country party-line telephone system originally had 8 on our line which grew to 14 over the years. The big box-like phone hung on the wall in the hall for privacy. We had to stand up when speaking. Our ring was three shorts *(Morse code for S).* The local general contractor on the line who got the most calls day and night had a call of one short and three longs *(Morse code for J)* and the operators sure knew how to keep us awake with incessant ringing.

The phone was right through the wall from my room.

The dad burn thing started ringing about 6am and rang constantly until about midnight. Perhaps that was why I slept with my head under the covers. Still do. We could call anyone on our line without going through the operator. When any call was finished we always gave one short ring as a ring off to let others know the line was free. Naturally, the busy bodies and those with long noses listened in, and knew all that was going on in the entire district. Some must have heard real juicy gossip to spread. These particular phones are now collectable relics.

ANGELS

Angels! Are there really such Beings?? As a child I thought so, although I didn't know what they were or what to call them. I still believe, although now I don't see them. However, as a child I could see them and talk to them, and being alone a lot of the time, I did. They were always understanding and gave good advice. There were always two or three with me when I played. I am sure, now that I am grown, that many of the things I did as a child must have been dangerous. And I feel equally sure that these dangers were thwarted by my Angels. If this sounds crazy so be it. I know I believe. How about you?? This little ditty comes to mind as I write this.

Four Angels by my bed, four Angels at my head,
One to watch, one to pray, and two to scare the Devil
away. Amen.

SCHOOL

Our school consisted of one room for all standards. *(See photo)* Our teacher was W. C. Collins. *(we called him Dunny, the N.Z. slang word for the outhouse - water closet).* He taught all 10 standards,

(Grades) Primers 1 - 4 and standards 1 - 6.

Later as the school numbers grew, a lady teacher was hired for the lower grades; Miss McAnly.. We all promptly fell in love with her. It was our solemn duty, especially as she was a good looking doll.

Collins was a good teacher, but was heavy with the strap. I was on his s… list. Never a day went by without my getting six of the best - on the hands - sometimes twice. *(He never made me cry - perhaps that was why he kept trying)*

Collins was of the Brethren church persuasion and he and Dad had many a discussion about religion. His belief was spare the rod and spoil the child. This view is fine in moderation. Today he would be in court for cruelty to children, as would a lot of teachers from that era.

Dad got very upset and disgusted over Collins's views and beliefs. He once told Dad that if someone broke into his house and violated his wife he would not try and stop the attack. He felt that if that happened it would be the will of God. Sick, Sick,

Miss McAnly believed in using the strap sparingly. She used it rarely, and only if some student had really been awfully naughty or downright disobedient. Those who got the strap from her *(I never did)* usually knew that they had it coming and forgave her.

When she did use it, she really laid it on. I remember my friend Fred was given six by her and he cried. Whether it was from shame or pain I never knew. Miss McAnly being single in a district like ours, with many eligible bachelors, meant that our dear teacher had plenty of swains. She was quickly courted and married. We boys all cried.

Six of the best. The only time I can remember why I received the strap, was when we were learning about fractions one day. We were asked for the two parts of a fraction. Someone said the top half was the numerator and I volunteered that the bottom half was the detonator. This unsolicited remark earned me six of the best for what was called insolence. Any excuse was enough to get my daily six.

Bookmaking - Illegal school activity. Perhaps one of the reasons that I was on Mr. Collins hit list was the fact that when his wife was expecting. I was taking one penny bets as to the future child's sex. His house was supplied and he lived only 50 yards from the school. He found out. Some big mouth tattled and was he horrified. As I said he was very religious. He complained to my Dad who smiled and said he would talk to me. He did, but it didn't amount to much of lecture. Secretly I think he was pleased that Collins's nose was out of joint. I do know that was the end of my bookmaking career and I never had to pay off. Come to think about it, it probably earned me at my daily six.

Making the ink for the school every week was in important job *(so I was told)* and each week I mixed the powder with water for the weekly ink supply. In the old days we used pens with nibs and ink that in the inkwells on the desk for writing. Pencils were not plentiful, and if we had one it was treasured.

Everyone in school knew the difference between a biplane and a monoplane. Airplanes were a rare thing in those days, especially where we were located. If we heard one, everyone in the school, was allowed outside to watch it fly over. Looking back it seems strange now as we never even look up if one flies over.

Early one morning just after sunrise I heard an airplane engine to the North of us. I listened. Suddenly heard an awful crash bang sound and then silence. I dismissed the incident from my mind. When I got to school that morning I found out there had been a collision between two planes one of which had crashed killing the pilot. The other plane had lost about ten feet of one wing but had somehow managed to land safely. Iris King, about 8 years old, had rushed to the scene, and the pilot had smiled at her and died in her arms as she had tried to help him. The crash had taken place right near her home. She stayed away from school that day. Later I visited the site after the authorities had removed all the parts and pieces they needed.

I had to walk nearly three miles to school every day. I usually had 45 minutes to make it. I had to be there by 9am. The teacher, *(Collins)* was a bit of a sadist and loved to use his large strap on the students who were late. Occasionally, when Dad could not be home for the midday feeding of the pigs, I had to run home and feed them, eating as I ran, and be back at school in an hour *(nearly a 6 mile round trip)* or risk another six of the best.

And today children think they have it tough if the bus is a few minutes late. I smile when I hear them complaining.

Phonetics. What we were taught, was the key to good diction and other related learning. We were taught the phonetic alphabet first before we learned the regular ABCs. This simple act of knowing that alphabet letters have two sounds has stood me in good stead throughout the years and in all of my future learning.

Children today don't seem to have the grasp of language as it is written, and as it sounds. To me English, as supposedly spoken by some, is literally absolute gibberish.

<u>Heating the Schoolhouse</u>. This was accomplished using a small wood burning stove. It was only fired up in in cold weather as we were expected to dress warmly, although more than fifty percent of the boys and girls did not wear shoes. They were just too expensive. I acquired my first real pair of good wearable shoes when I was about fourteen. All the boys wore short pants about 4 inches above the knees, and the girls of course wore dresses below the knees. We had an old pine stump, full of sticky gum, that gave us chips for a starter and we all scouted about for wood. No wood - no fire.

<u>Rote Learning</u>.   Learning the multiplication tables through 12 X 12 and having contests to see who could recite them most quickly. I loved history, mathematics, reading, writing, and geography. Still do. Hated geometry and English with all the verbs, dangling participles, adjectives objects, etc. It must have stuck however. Today I pride myself on my command of the language and on my ability to speak and be understood, and to speak correctly. *(Dig my diction?)*   No doubt about it; the teaching methods used then have stood me in good stead over the years.

<u>My education</u>, while poor by some standards, was, in many cases, better than those who have some college instruction under their belt. Some people educated abroad, say that good English hasn't been spoken in the U.S.A. for years. I must admit that when I first joined the US army, shortly after my arrival, I did have trouble with the deep Southern accent.

School projects. I wrote three. "Scenic New Zealand", "The British Isles" and "World War Two," a total of 3 separate volumes which I still have hidden away. These projects were designed to teach us to research and learn about the countries we were writing about.

The many hours I put into these projects were well worth it. For each, I was rewarded with a book prize from the schoolmaster. with a "very well done." Those magic words again.

Some the children I went to school with. The Ryan Twins; Tony & Basil *(my best friends)* and their sister Alicia *(now a Catholic nun.)*, Betty Glanville, and her brothers Stanley *(committed suicide),* and Norman *(went insane),* John Krippner, Bertie, Daphne, and Iris King, Herbert Becker, Desmond Stoney, Freddie Brokenshire *(dead at 21)* and his sister Merle *(Hicks),* two Hannah boys and their sister Olive, Bill Hawkes.

There were others but I do not remember them. I lost track of everyone after I moved away from home to make my fortune.

As Wainui was a farming community, many of the young people stayed home on the family land as have their children.

To look at me now you would never believe that I once danced the light fantastic. Pretty good too. We all had to take part in the recreational aspects of the school's curriculum. Folk dancing was part of it as was acting, reading etc. I really enjoyed learning and doing. My dancing partner was Betty on whom I had a secret crush.

The school kept a record of the daily rainfall and each day someone was chosen to read the gauge and record the amount. I wonder if they still do.

Steeple-chasing. This was a yearly school race over

all sorts of obstacles such as fences, streams, trees, bogs etc. It was usually up the side of a fairly steep hill and down again winding through the countryside and the various obstacles. The distance was about 5 miles. We trained, by running up the side of a large nearby hill near to the school.

On the day of the race time many of the local population and parents came to urge us on and cheer for us. I always came in second. I never could, no matter how hard I trained, beat my training buddy Sydney Drinnan. He was only a little chap too. Good stuff is done up in small parcels.

The one school chum that I would really like to meet again. Although we were not real good cobbers, (friends) I always felt an empathy for John Krippner. His father often kept him at the cowshed doing chores, with the result that he was nearly always late for school. Collins usually gave him six of the best because of it, and the strap hurt him so badly that he would cry for a long time. My heart went out to him for being punished for something beyond his control. He also suffered from epileptic fits on rare occasions, which were not really understood in those days.

Thankfully we have progressed mightily in that field of knowing more about children's behavior problems. I have lost track of him, and all others, but heard that he went on to make something of himself and eventually overcame the epilepsy. I would really enjoy meeting him again one day.

My cobber Fred came from a fairly well off farming family and as a result had lunches that I only dreamt about. Strangely, he wanted what I had and so we swapped. Often a cheese and jam, date, or baloney sandwich was traded for several chocolate cookies, or a piece of good looking cake. His family had enough money to buy these goodies, we did not, so it was a rare treat for me. I often thought that he got the best of the deal as I was always hungry for the rest of the day. Notwithstanding, I still swapped. Perhaps all the rich food his family ate was the cause of his death at age 21.

REGGIE CARTER'S ORCHARD

Stealing *(pinching or nicking)* fruit from Reggie Carter's Orchard. Every day on the way home from school during the fruit season, I had to walk by trees laden with nice ripe red apples. The temptation was just too much for a young boy with all those succulent juicy red or golden apples hanging on the trees, just waiting to be picked and eaten.

The apples would call to me. *"Come and eat us. We are so good. Try us - you will like us."* I would sneak in and pinch *(steal)* a few.

Sometimes mean grumpy ole Reggie Carter would be waiting and would run me off. He would then call my Dad and complain. Dad would lecture me *(in one ear and out the other).* As I said the temptation was just too great. Those tempting apples would make my taste buds titillate. The apples would call to me again, and a few days later I would do what any red-blooded young boy would do. Give right in o temptation and sneak into the orchard and pinch a few more. Somehow, the apples always tasted so much better than the ones we grew in our own orchard, or the ones we bought from Reggie Carter. Probably still would.

FIGHT AT KING'S GARAGE

The fight at the *(OK)* King's garage. I had been

challenged to a fight by a kid quite a bit older than I. Sydney Jarvis, who was only in the area for several years, had made my life miserable with his tormenting and mouthing off. Finally I could take no more. "OK, Let us fight it out", I said finally. Inside King's garage, a large garage where trucks were repaired and parked. After school was the chosen time and place of combat. Many of the local children came to watch as did several adults who worked close by. We squared off and went at it. All sorts of punches, kicks etc. were traded. Anything was legal. I never knew who won, if anyone. I was more respected after that however and no one else messed with me. When Dad found out about the fight *(he could see the results on me)* he asked who had won. "I don't know," I said. "Well you go back to school tomorrow and make sure that you win this time," he said, "or I, will give you a spanking when you get home." I don't remember if we ever did fight again. Jarvis moved on shortly afterwards. As far as I was concerned it was good riddance.

HOME GUARD UNIT

During the early part of W.W.2, when the tide of the war looked ominous and there was a distinct possibility that we could and might be invaded by Japanese forces. The local farmers formed a home guard unit, of which my Dad was a part.

They practiced drilling, shooting, field maneuvers. *(Both night and day)* In general they had a pretty good time. At least they were not working. Dad told us that one day while they were drilling near an old quarry that was full of water, he was asked to give the commands. Well, he got the men going straight for the cliff overlooking the water and couldn't remember the proper command to stop or wheel them. The chief instructor watched and finally yelled, *"For God's sake Arthur say something, even if it's only goodbye boys."*

Everyone laughed of course and my Dad's turn was over. He was a better farmer than soldier.

BIRDS & THE BEES

Shortly after turning sixteen my stepmother gave me a talk about the birds and the bees *(?? her version)* about which I still laugh. I was in the bathroom/laundry washing my face and hands when she happened in. To the best of my recollection this is what she said.

"Peter you are sixteen now and you will have to be careful around the girls. We don't want to have be paying support for a child for the next 16 years."

With at she swept regally out of the room while I just stood there open mouthed wondering what that was all about. When I realized what she had said I burst out laughing. I am still laughing to this day.

MEAT AND BUTTER

Our meat and butter, which we sometimes churned, and anything else that needed to be kept cool was stored in the safe, which was about 2 feet X 3 feet. It protruded out of the north wall of the house in the small kitchen. Three sides were open, covered with fly proof gauze to allow any breeze we had to waft through. Cold meat stayed O.K. for about two days. Butter somewhat longer. Milk of course we had every day being a dairy farm.

Cream, even though we produced it, was a treat. Cream was our cash crop. Flies and food spoilage were severe problems and great care was taken.
To help control the fly problem *(there were no window screens)* fly catcher papers were used in many homes. They were about 15" long and about 1" wide and were covered with some sort of sticky goo. They were hung at strategic locations throughout the house. When the fly or other flying pest landed on it they were stuck and died. You can imagine what they were like if left unchanged for a few days. However, they were very effective.

BICYCLE

Dirt poor. We were so poor that even mice didn't live with us. I used to wonder what it would be like to have any money to spend and what I would buy. There were so many things I wanted; so many things I didn't have. All I remember is that a NEW bike was on the top of the list along with some chocolate chip cookies.

My new bicycle wasn't really new, but it was new to me. I was now able to ride to school and be a part of the other children who also had bikes. I often wondered where my Dad got the few shillings it cost to buy it. My first motorcycle only cost 200 shillings - L15-0-0, about $45.00 in those days. Keeping the tires patched and the hubs and brakes working was an experience that has served to keep me doing and fixing all my life, so far.

(Just ask my children or my grandchildren. If anything breaks Papa will fix it.) If the bike broke down I had to walk to school so I learned to fix it rather than walk.

FISHING FOR WHALES

Fishing for Whales at Pettit's Waitoki *(Why-toe-key)* lime works. Sometimes my Dad worked for a few days at the lime works and he took me along. There was a creek nearby and I asked to be allowed to fish. My Dad said, "OK but watch out for the really large fish that's in there. If he gets hold of the line he may drag you into the creek."

Hardly daring to breathe, I baited the bent pin with a worm put the line into the water, and wrapped my arms around a fence post for safety and waited for the big fish to strike. Of course, it never did. Dad and the fellow workers looked over at me and saw my safety precautions. It sure did cause some merriment. Somehow, I felt betrayed, and it was a long time before I fished again.

LONG PANTS

Pants; short ones that had patches on the patches on the patches. When I was a boy none of the schoolboys wore long pants or shoes or boots either. Long pants were the mark of a man. New pants were a rare thing and being a tough kid, if I got any they didn't stay new for long much to the exasperation of my Dad and stepmother.   Shirts were the same. *(Underwear, what was that?)*   Going up I never had any such finery as underwear although I had heard that some sissy city people wore it.

THE BULL

<u>The taming of the Bull</u>. I was about 10 when Dad remarried. He went away for a week on holiday, and I was left in charge, which included doing all the work.   Dad must have thought that I could it and I didn't want to disappoint him.   Several days after Dad had gone, our bull *(nasty brute)* caught me in the small yard by the cowshed, charged me, knocking me down. I was very lucky not to be gored.

He had caught me squarely with middle of his head with a horn going on either side of me.   I was somewhat stunned but recovered quickly.   My dog Scottie, at my frantic command, distracted him long enough for me to escape.

"We can't have this" I thought. *"How to tame him. I want revenge on this bull for attacking me. I know, Dehorning* (cutting off his horns) *is a good thought. No, that might kill him if I do it wrong. Castrate him. No that is not an option as we need him. Darn bull* is dangerous."   Think Peter, think. *"Use your head. Think it through. What would Dad do?"*

Then it hit me. I knew what I must do.   Armed with a long heavy stick, and with the help of the dog, I forced the bull into the yard and into a stall in the cowshed. Then I put the chain across his rear and tied his rear feet together *(no mean feat for a youngster)*. I then carefully tied up his head to keep the horns out of the way, to make what I planned to do, easier.

Then the fun began. I took a piece of steel with a sharp point and put a hole through the middle part of his nose *(naturally the bull objected, but the roping held firm)*. Then I put in a copper bull ring specially made for this very purpose *(we just happened to have one)* about 5" in diameter, held together be a tiny screw, into the hole in his nose. I then attached, with baling wire, a 12 foot length of a horse trace chain to the ring, untied him, and let him go. He soon learned to walk with his head to one side to avoid stepping on the chain.

Revenge complete, or so I thought. Several days went by. I didn't see the bull. "Where could he be I wondered? I hope he is O.K." I went out looking for him and there he was. The chain was stuck to a tree root, held by the hook on the end of the chain I had forgotten to remove. All the grass had been eaten down as far as he could reach. He was beaten.

Now I faced a problem "Should I risk trying to let him go? I must find a way to let him go. What if he tries to attack me again? Here goes nothing. I must risk it. As I walked toward him his head dropped in a gesture of utter submission. He was thirsty and hungry. I went and carefully unhooked the chain and led him home like a puppy. I then took the hook off the end of the chain and then let him have drink of water. He had been about three days without one.

"Revenge complete." I felt so superior. What a great feeling. I had battled the beast and won. He was a really docile bull after that.

When Dad came home we caught him and shortened the chain to 2 feet to keep him that way. Again, I heard those wonderful words, "Well done lad."

BRINGING IN THE COWS

I stayed warm on colder days by running and staying active. Sometimes I would make the dog sit while I played his part and ran out into the meadow to bring in the cows. I suppose the dog thought I was crazy to do his job, but in those days I could really run and it was a good way to keep warm. In spite of the hardships I was healthy, and the soles of my bare feet were like the soles of leather shoes.

TURNIPS, SWEDES, & ICE CREAM

Turnips and Swedes. *(Rutabagas)* We grew these for the cattle. Sometimes as I went through the field I would pull up several, take a handful of leaves and wring off the rest. I now had a handle. I would peel with my teeth *(dirt notwithstanding)* and proceed to enjoy. Right from Mother Nature herself.
Ice cream cones. When we went to Auckland, which was only about twice a year, I was treated to an ice cream cone. What a treat.

WATER TANK

Cleaning out the house drinking water tank. During a really dry spell it was my chore to get into the water tank and clean it out of anything that had fallen in since the last cleaning. The tank had no lid. All household water was caught from runoff from the house roof. If there was no rain, we were able to refill the tank from the cistern at the top of the hill by the house. This cistern was kept full by pumping the water from a spring. The cistern water also fed the cowshed.

In the bottom of the tank I would often find all sorts of things such as twigs, sometimes even dead birds, mice and rats etc. The drain pipe from the tank to the house was about nine inches from the tank bottom for this very reason. No one ever seemed to worry and we never seemed to suffer as a result. Perhaps the mixture was an elixir that kept us healthy!! Perhaps the health department should check into this, there may be something here of value along nutritional lines. Of course, water boiled for tea was OK. However, we did drink the water. We never did put a cover on that tank.

GOING TO AUCKLAND

Tate's motor bus service. Whenever we wanted to go to Auckland we had to rely on Tate's bus service. It went every day through Silverdale, a five mile walk away, and through Wainui corners, which was a bit over a mile away twice a week. We always called and let them know to pick us up. Sort of like a super taxi service.

Crossing the harbor to Auckland. All vehicles going into Auckland from the North-shore had to use the vehicular ferry boats. There were also passenger ferry boats. *(Bet you didn't know they had their own navy.)*

The ferries ran quite often and the trip took about 20 minutes. Motor cycles were always allowed on first to fill up spots where vehicles could not be placed. Today there is an eight lane bridge over the harbor; no waiting.

When first constructed, the original harbor bridge was only four lanes wide and was out of date before it was even finished. The government then decided to widen it. Experts were called in from the UK and the USA. None of their engineers would commit to attempt the widening. The Japanese engineers were called in, and promptly attacked the problem. They built two extra lanes on each side, widening the bridge to eight lanes. The project was dubbed 'The Nippon Clip-on.' The passenger boats still run.

FISH & CHIPS & HOT JAM

As children we called them "Chish and Fipps" instead of fish and chips. Another treat if Dad went to town and we didn't. Good even when cold or warmed over. Yum!!

Smoked fish. In New Zealand, smoked Schnapper, is *(or was)* a regular staple in the diet of city people. At our house, whenever we bought some, it was simmered in milk and garnished with butter and parsley for a treat that I would still enjoy. Also good eaten cold without further cooking. Step-mother had to watch me when we had it or it would be gone.

One day I came into the kitchen where step-mother had just set out some jam tarts from the oven. They looked scrumptious. I picked up one and poured the runny jam onto my tongue. It was hot, just out of the oven and I had a sore burnt tongue for days. "Serves you right, that will teach you" was the only consolation I got from stepmother.

WEEKLY BATH

Taking our weekly bath. *(Whether we needed it or not!! - we always did!!)* The three girls bathed first, then Stepmother, then me, then Dad. It was quite an experience. Poor Dad - he got the worst of it but at least we got some of the grime off. During the warmer weather Dad and I sometimes went to the creek with a bar of homemade lye soap, a bucket and a towel, for a wash down. A bucket of cold water, soap up, another bucket of cold water, towel off, dress and we were done. When we got electricity and had hot water at the cowshed, we had our wash-downs there. I used to really enjoy the time spent with my Dad on these intimate occasions.

GOLDEN SYRUP

Chelsea Honey *(Golden syrup)* is a product made from sugar cane. Made by refining treacle another step until it was golden brown in color. It came in a Billy-can; about 7 lbs. in weight. The empty Billy-can *(about a quart)* was sometimes used in the bush to brew tea, a handle having been added for convenience. The name "Chelsea Honey" was used because the product was refined in the New Zealand township of Chelsea.

Golden syrup tarts and pies were a big thing then, as the product was cheap and tasted great if you liked sweet things. This product is still available in some stores throughout the U.S.A.

HARVEST TIME

At the start of the harvesting season Dad would give me a sack with about a dozen quart bottles of beer. *(There was a saying that I still subscribe to - If you could not drink a quart you were not thirsty)* to put into the creek to keep them cool. When the hay was all in, Dad would nod to me and I would run and fetch the beer, one bottle for each worker.
Dad allowed me to take a swallow or two when I was younger, but what a feeling of pride I had when Dad

pronounced me old enough to have a bottle of my own *(I was about 14)*. After a hot day in the harvest field it sure tasted good, and probably still would come to think about it.

One year during the harvest season I was stabbed accidentally just above the left knee with a pitchfork prong. While it was painful, no one thought much about it until several days later when I got sick and my groin became swollen. I was taken to Doctor Matheson in Helensville. He allowed me to watch. I was fascinated with all gadgets the doctor had and was laying out.

He made about a 1 ½ inch incision over the swelling and then put a small tray under my leg. A pair of tongs were inserted into the wound and opened up. Out gushed the pus. Cleanup and several stitches, a bandage, and he was all done. I was O.K. in about a week, but very leery around pitchforks.

TIN ROOF

During the cold, windy and rainy nights I would snuggle down into the soft down mattress and cover everything to keep toasty warm. I still like to cover my ears while sleeping. I have heard that the ears are the body's thermostat.

The rain, pounding on the tin roof, was like relaxing music that lulled me to sleep. I still like the musical sound of heavy rain on a tin roof and love a storm with lightning and thunder. One of Heaven's musical masterpieces. Because of the rough house construction, there were little gaps in the walls that the air came through when it was windy, and the sacking *(called scrim)* which was tacked onto the walls and covered with wallpaper would bulge out from the walls. I used to dread the 4 a.m. call from my Dad to get up and get the cows in on these occasions. I vowed if ever I was on my own I would sleep in, and now I do, sometimes until the crack of 9 a.m.

MILKING TIME

Four o'clock in the morning. *("Time to get up son")*

"It is now time to go out and succeed in extracting from the feminine gender of the bovine species, that luscious and nutritious white substance known as milk."

Four a.m. was the usual time to rise and get the cows into the shed, regardless of the inclement *weather (it was often raining).* On frosty cold mornings my feet would soon be like ice blocks *(I never had a pair of shoes or boots until I was about 13 or 14).* To try and warm my cold feet, I would stand where the cows had been laying or find a nice newly dropped cow pie and stand in it, relishing the warmth as the fresh warm manure oozed between my toes. Don't laugh, there was nothing else available to keep the tootsies warm. *(Seems like a long time ago now.)*

When the cows were in the shed and I had washed my feet off *(see, I did wash them)* Dad would have nice hot coffee with liquid chicory ready. I can taste it to this day! When the first milk came through the pipes we would add some to the hot coffee and drink. There was usually a large sandwich, or a large piece of fruit cake to tide us over as breakfast which would not be eaten until around 8a.m., 4 hours later.

Very occasionally Dad would leave me the alarm clock and give me a short break. How I relished the extra sack time. I was careful not to be late knowing would spoil any future respites.

As soon as I opened the back door in the morning at 4 a.m., the dog was on his feet whining to be let off the chain and go to work. As we walked toward the shed with him at my heels, I would try and judge how long it would take me to walk to the paddock gate. I knew the dog wouldn't take long to have the cows rounded up and waiting.

As soon as I said *"go get 'em"* he was off like shot. How he ever saw on those pitch-black mornings I will never know. I know I couldn't. Knowing the way was a big help however as I had no torch *(aka flashlight)*.

When I arrived at the gate all the cows were always there and waiting. I would open the gate and lead the herd to the cowshed, the dog following the cows and taking care of any stragglers. Very occasionally, later at daylight, when we counted heads, one cow would be missing *(our dog didn't miss very often)*. I would send the dog out to bring the culprit in. He usually brought her in at full gallop, nipping at her heals, as if teaching her a lesson; don't mess with me again, I have been insulted. Not too many cows tried for seconds believe me.

SCOTTIE
Faithful Dog and Friend

To see the dog literally jump through mud that was deeper than his legs were long, was a sight to behold. His only rewards for all his untiring work were a dish of milk, the sludge from the separator bowl at wash-up time, table scraps and a pat on the head. He was a great worker and a good pal to me. His name was Scottie. I hope there is a doggie heaven - if there is, he should be there. I have often wondered what a dog like he was, was worth monetarily. There were other canine friends that worked the farm with us over the years. Glen and Ring were two, but none held a place in my boyhood heart like Scottie.

When Scottie died, I cried. Our next dog was Glen. Glen was a sheep dog leader and always went for the cow's head instead of the hind end. When we finally broke him of the habit and trained him to go for the hind end he would leap up and bite the cows on the tail. Sometimes it was a bit bloody. He had to be cured but how. I solved it partially by putting one of his front legs through the neck collar forcing him to run on three legs. He staggered about for a bit but soon learned to hop about. When he got used to that leg being up I would change legs.

It didn't take him long to be almost as fast on three legs as he was on four, but he just couldn't jump and do any damage although he tried. I remember that he once went missing chasing a rabbit with his foot still in his collar. When he didn't return home I was quite upset. He was gone for several days and came home limping on his three good legs. The one that had been in the collar has stiffened up and I had to take off the collar to let it become useful again.

He was as good as new in a couple of days but never overcame his desire to chase rabbits while on duty. We didn't keep him very long. Dad sold him to a neighbor.

MIRO TREE

We had only one Miro tree on our farm. If the bark of the Miro tree was slashed and the sap allowed to run, the dark blood red liquid was a good poultice for severe wounds, cuts and abrasions. It was used quite extensively by the Maoris and early European settlers, who prized it for the healing properties. I also used it many times for wounds and scrapes.

THE FIVE SISTERS

Splitting posts and fence battens. Working in the bush, splitting timber with Dad was always enjoyable. Posts were cut or split from Puriri (*Poo-ri-ree*) and the battens were usually split from Tanekaha *(Tan-e-ka-ha.)* Dad had an eagle eye and very seldom missed when splitting smaller pieces. It was during these times that Dad taught me how to use an axe, a mall and wedges, how to fall timber where he wanted it, and the names of the various native trees and their uses. Dad was very wise and knew a great deal about the various native fauna.

When working in the bush we always took tucker *(food)* along. At lunch time it was my job to boil the Billy-can and make the tea. It was during these times in the bush that I learned the art making a hot fire quickly. My Dad was an excellent woodsman and taught me many things about fire making and the art of survival that I have been able to make good use of in later years when camping out.

The five sisters *(so called)* were a group of five large Puriri trees which we cut down and split into fence posts. They were large splendid specimens that grew in an area about 20 square feet in the back bush. Dad agonized about cutting them as they were quite unique, but finally did as we needed both posts and the money they could be sold for. Puriri posts were very much in demand as they never decayed or rotted, even when in the ground for twenty years or more. *(Today pressure treated pine is used)*

The left over pieces were an excellent source of firewood, creating a very hot fire for a long time, due to the denseness of the wood. Nothing was wasted, the limbs and smaller branches were cut up for firewood. From then on we always referred to that area simply as "the five sisters."

In 1976 I visited New Zealand and took my two daughters for a tour of the farm where I grew up. I don't know what they expected to see when we visited the area of the five sisters. All they were able to see were the five stumps. I think they experienced a let-down after all I had said about the spot. In my mind's eye, I can still see those magnificent specimens of the Puriri trees as they were before they were cut down.

TEA TIME

Teatime. The Billy-can was an empty Golden Syrup can *(about a quart)* to which a wire handle had been attached. When the water boiled the tea was put in and the water allowed to continue boiling for about 30 seconds. It was then taken off the fire and the side of the Billy-can was gently tapped with a small twig to settle the tea leaves. Sugar and milk was then added and the tea was ready. Boy, did it ever taste good. So did the tucker *(food)* to a growing lad.

When boiling water it was very important to lay a small green twig across the top of the Billy-can to prevent the water from having a smoky taste. After we had eaten Dad would have a smoke and would then lie down for about 30 minutes and rest. As a boy I always thought it was a good idea. Still is.
I will always remember Dad as a friend
who really loved me.

TWO HORSE TEAM

Often, when we were working, and the job Dad was doing was too much for me, Dad would have me drive the two horse team, which I had learned to do at a very early age. I remember I had to stand on an old box to be able to put the horse Collar and Haymes around the horse's necks.

I would take loads out to the road on the 'CAT' *(catamaran)* and unload it. It was hard work for a boy, but I was proud to be of help. Then I would come back for another load. Talk about tired at the end of the day. It felt good though, and Dad's encouragement always made me feel better. "Well done boy" was his favorite saying, a saying that I never tired of hearing.

Today there are probably very few adult farmers who can plough with a hand held moldboard plough. I learned early and did a lot of ploughing during my early years. It was hard work, a lot of fun, and there was always a good feeling to know I had done well.

Once when I was about twelve, Dad and stepmother took a rare much earned short vacation. I decided to plow what we called 'Marble Hill.' I started at the bottom and worked up, going round and round.

It is noteworthy that there were a lot of seashells in the ploughed sod. Perhaps the area was once covered as a result of 'the flood' or a more recent flood. When Dad returned I again heard those wonderful words of praise.

HAY-SWEEP

One year I worked in the harvest field for my

neighbor Selwyn Lloyd, manning the hay-sweep. This was full grown man's job, but at age 16 as I was able to do it I was encouraged to continue. I earned the magnificent sum of 1/6 an hour (about 18 cents). I knew the other workers *(men)* earned much more. However, I was determined to prove my worth, and to show that I too was grown up. I guess I was just too dumb to realize what a fool I must have made of myself The Lloyd's hay-baler was horse powered using an old horse that walked around and around powering a hay-goose and hay rammer. With it we were able to bale about 12 bales an hour. It was only used for one season as it was painfully slow and horribly out of date. All the new-fangled hay balers had a gasoline engine. Next year he purchased one.

THINGS OF THE SEA

Paua seashells when polished are used in the manufacture of jewelry. Sea Urchins, a spinney shell, round with flattened ends was prized by us children for decorative purposes. When found, great care to be taken not to touch them or disturb the pool. If we did, they had a way of sticking their spines to the rock and we would be unable to get them off. We had to sneak our hand into the pool and grab and pull at the same time before the sticking process was activated. They were left in the sun until the interior was dead. Then they were washed out, dried and decorated. We had a lot of fun when we went to the beach scrambling in the rocks to find them.

Pippies, Mussels, Cockles. These were some of the shellfish found around the coasts. Good eating, especially when steamed. A Pippie is just like a small oyster in size.

Toheroas. (Papjoes-ventricosa) is another species of

shellfish with green meat and was/is highly prized for taste. Minced up they make great soup or patties. I distinctly remember digging for them on the beach, just out of Waiuku. Knowing they were protected *(even then)* made me very careful not to exceed the limit. This particular shellfish is still protected *(the Ministry of Fishing now allows only one day a year for harvesting)* and it is a highly prized delicacy. The white man is limited to twelve; there is no limit for the native Maoris.

NATIVE BUSH - Trees and Flax

Nikau Palm Treea.. This graceful palm has proven to be food for the birds who love the berries it produces. As mentioned earlier, the palm fronds were used as roofing on the Whare when platted together. When felled and the frond part split open, the very center part of about 3 inches in diameter is an edible portion and was quite a treat when we were growing up. The edible part was quite crunchy, with a taste somewhat like raw potato.

I heard stories, as I was growing up, about settlers in the early days who became lost in the bush and died of starvation with all that good food right there. Unfortunately, the tree must be chopped down, killing it. A life for a life. I would never starve in the New Zealand bush. This edible portion and water will sustain anyone for long periods of time.

Flax grew abundantly where I was raised, in lower areas and swampy land. The flower stalks and leaves grow tall, up to about 10', and we used the leaves as a rough rope source. The native Maoris used flax as a source for basket weaving and clothing.

Te-Tanu, the giant Kauri trees. The natives called the

96

giant Kauri trees Te-Tanu *(gods of the forest)*. This particular tree is probably related to the California Redwood. Unfortunately, nearly all the giant ones are gone. Truly a tribute to man's greed.

I remember growing up and seeing the large partially burned out stumps of large trees that had probably been cut and harvested around the turn of the 20th century These burnt out stumps were so big that I used to hide inside their burnt out shells and plink away at rabbits with my .22 rifle.

There was also evidence of pit saw operations, used to cut these large trees into pieces for easier handling after the tree was down. A pit was dug under the trunk long-ways. A two-man saw, one man on top of the log pulled the saw up and the saw-man in the pit pulled it down, going down the length of the trunk cutting the trunk into flitches *(large pieces)l* These pieces were then easier to handle, and probably moved about by bullock teams. It must have been hot dusty work for the poor guy in the pit. History records that many of the smaller trees were used for ship masts due to the absence of branches, sometimes up to eighty feet with no knots.

The Lloyd's Giant Kauri tree. This magnificent majestic Kauri tree towers away above the surrounding bush growth. It is over 90' to the first limb. Truly one of the last magnificent trees called Te-Tanu. The circumference measures *(1976)* over 25 feet. Close up, this god of the forest was truly magnificently awesome to behold. I know, I stood under it many times. It is my prayer, and the prayer of all who have seen it, that this tree, and others like it, will never be destroyed. I know this one is safe as long as the Lloyd family owns it. It should be declared a national monument if it hasn't been already.   It is surrounded by several acres of bush as a buffer.

Recently I received word that this magnificent tree, and several acres of surrounding bush has been dedicated to the New Zealand Plant Conservation Network. PTL

WEEDS & HARD WORK

Gorse, Thistles, Buttercup, Blackberries, Rushes - of all these weed problems Gorse is one of a real farmer's ongoing pests, being very prolific grower. Several years ago, while I was in Scotland, I noticed quite a lot of this pest. It must be constantly be grubbed out, stacked and burned. It seems as if it has a charmed life. Grubbing was a job we all did very carefully due to the large thorns that covered the mature plant.

Originally, not a part of New Zealand's native plant life, some idiot do-gooders actually planted rows and rows gorse with idea of using the tender young sprouting shoots for cattle fodder. However, once the plant starts to mature, and the protective thorns begin to sprout, and no animal is crazy enough to go near it.

One morning after breakfast, Dad told me to take my lunch and the mattock and go out into the fields to grub gorse, and thistles until afternoon milking time. With my trusty mattock, my tucker bag and my pal the dog, away I went. I left the house at about 8:30 a.m. I worked hard all morning, occasionally looking at the sky like my Dad did. This was his way of determining the time. I finally decided it was lunch time. After eating, and having a rest to let my tucker settle, I went back at it. I worked all afternoon and was feeling really tired after such a hard day of work. I had even raised a good sweat and felt really good about having done so much work all on my own. After checking the sun in the sky again, I decided it was almost afternoon milking time. I headed home for a quick afternoon snack before going out for the cows. Imagine my consternation when I discovered it was only 11.30 am.

How my Dad laughed and laughed. He talked about it for years. The good part was that I was not sent back out by myself. Dad came with me, and this time I put in a full day.

FATHER'S FORGIVENESS

One morning, while I was away over towards the middle of the farm, putting the cows into the right paddock, Dad started shouting instructions. I must have been in a bad mood, or crazy, because I yelled back to him,

"What do you want you silly old fool." Whoops!! Now I knew I was in big trouble. When I realized the enormity of what I had said, and the possible inevitable outcome, I was transfixed to the spot, and overcome with a fearful remorse. In those days *(how times have changed)* children had a very profound respect for their parents and elders and never back chatted or criticized them, due to the consequences. I knew that I was in deep doo-doo!!

Rather than face the consequences I decided to run away from home right then. The only problem was, to where? I went over the hill and sat down with the dog, who was always most understanding and seemed most concerned that I had a problem. I struggled to plan my course of action. Time passed. I agonized.

Suddenly there was Dad coming toward me. I sprang to my feet ready to take to my scrapers. I couldn't let him get me. I would surely rue the day. But Dad was smiling. Uh oh! Was this some new ploy to get me? I knew that if he got hold of me I would surely rue the day I had been born. I also knew I could outrun him as he had that bad leg.

"I think you are sorry for what you said," he said. *"Come on home with me and have some breakfast."* Magic words. Food. I was off the hook. He put his arm around my shoulders and we walked to the house for a late breakfast.

What a great Dad I had to be sure.

EVENINGS AROUND THE FIRE

Our fire was the only source of heat in the house. Sometimes friends would come over and we would listen to good music *(78 RPM on the wind up by hand gramophone.)* Other times we would listen to the radio shows on our Golden Knight radio. My favorites were 'The Green Hornet', 'Out of the Silence', 'The Air Adventures of Jimmie Allen', 'The Lone Ranger' and 'The Shadow.'

How, as a young man, I thrilled as the radio made all these wonderful characters really come alive. I used to sit glued to the spot whenever these programs were on. Remember, my world was really small in those bygone days. I was also exposed to a lot of good music *(classical)* during those early years. I am still what some call a long hair, as I still like the classics. However, there was one American program that Dad simply could not stand due to the horrible high-pitched squeaky voice Jane used in the program 'Jane Ace.' I didn't like it either. Other times we would get comfortable by the fire and read *(we did a lot of it)* or do home-work from school.

A BIBLE WORD

A Bible word, Explanation and Incomprehensible Understanding!! My stepmother often read the Bible aloud while we listened. One evening while reading, she pronounced a word 'War-eeze.' Dad stopped her and asked her to spell it. She did 'w-h-o-r-e-s.' Dad chuckled and pronounced it correctly.

"What does it mean," my stepmother asked.

"Well," said my father, *"it is a woman who sells herself sexually for money."*

"Oh!" said mother, now really confused. A deadly pregnant silence followed her remark. *"How could any woman do such a thing?"* she asked in an incredulous voice, now thoroughly nonplussed, and at a loss for words or understanding. Being locally raised, she knew nothing of the world outside of our locally geographic area.

As a family we sat around, and while Dad explained it to us all, along with some of the other things that went on in the outside world. Perhaps a few more family discussions would be in order in today's so called modern society.

DAD & RECENT HISTORY

Dad told us history stories that were reasonably recent history to him. His life span was from 1900 to 1968.

- When the first man flew the English Channel in an aero-plane - Louis Baleriot *(July 19ᵗʰ 1909)* Dad was 8 ½ years old.
- The massacre of the 146 prisoners in the black hole of Calcutta *(6/20/1756)*
- The charge of the light Brigade in the Crimean war *(Oct 25ᵗʰ 1854)*.
- The Boer War in South Africa. *(November 11ᵗʰ 1899)*
- The sinking of the Titanic *(April 15ᵗʰ 1912)* Dad was not 12 yet.
- Custer last stand *(June 25ᵗʰ 1878)*
- Stories from World War One were also recent history. He also thrilled us with many other stories from around the world and their cultures.
- Stories about New Zealand,
- Stories about the Maoris, their culture and the wars when the first white settlers arrived. How when we grew up, what was expected of us.

NAME THAT SPOT

Most of the places on the farm had names so that we could identify where something was happening, or where something was. i.e.

- **Marble hill**, where I had recently ploughed.
- The **Old lime heap**, where several bags of lime had been spilled.
- **Kauri ridge,** where a lot of timber had been harvested.

- **Handcuff bush**, where I had had an adventure.
- **Blind gully**, a place where one had to be close-up to see the area.
- **The Five Sisters**, the home of the large fallen Puriri trees.
- **Jimmy's paddocks.**
- **Joan's swimming Hole**, where my cousin Joan had recently had a swim.
- **The Pump paddock,** the source of our water supply.
- **The Home paddock**, by the house.
- **The Back flats** at the rear of the farm, etc.

APPENDICITIS

On day while the men were working at the neighbor's sawmill, Dad fell the ground moaning and clutching his stomach. The neighbor's son, Mervyn walked by, looked down and said, "What's the matter Arthur, having a baby." Even as a young lad, I wanted to hit this unfeeling goon for being so callus and unfeeling, but he was grown and I was only a boy. Dad was taken to the local doctor and had his appendix removed. I ran the farm for a few days while Dad recovered. The neighbor's son was later killed when a tree fell on him. I did not mourn.

JOAN'S SWIMMING HOLE

One summer my cousin Joan Harnett *(Married Dunsmuir - now deceased)* came to visit. We were over at the back flat at the bottom of Kauri Ridge where there is a creek. At one place the creek widened to a good size pond. *(At least it used to)* Joan decided to take a dip. She swam well, and I was impressed. From that day forward this particular spot was known as Joan's swimming hole.

Joan's swimming hole was where I learned to swim. One day Dad threw me in and walked away saying "swim or drown." I learned to swim really fast. Later I realized that Dad was watching me over his shoulder just in case.

MY FIRST SUIT AND SHOES

I was nearly fourteen when Dad took me to the Farmer's Trading Company in Auckland *(a large General store)* and fitted me out with a light blue pinstriped suit with long pants *(My first pair)* a shirt with two detachable collars, collar stud, tie, socks and shoes *(no underwear)*. Talk about a transformation from the ugly duckling. I remember how I felt all dressed up like a prize turkey. As we walked out of the store, I remember telling Dad that everyone was looking at me. He smiled and said they weren't, and neither they were of course, but I really felt that they were. I was so self-conscious. That outfit lasted me a long time.

NIKAU, KUMERAHO, SULFUR, TREACLE, & BOILS

Nikau trees. This graceful palm proves to be food for the birds who love the berries it produces. As mentioned earlier, the palm fronds were used as roofing on the Whare when platted together. When felled and the frond part split open, the edible portion was quite a treat when we were growing up. I would never starve in the New Zealand bush. This edible portion and water will sustain you for long periods of time.
Kumeraho, a low growing shrub with purpled green

leaves. It smelled like an overripe outhouse ugh! We used it as a tonic. The leaves of this wild plant were boiled, strained, cooled and the liquid drunk. The taste was bitter in the mouth for a start; *(tasted like snake oil)* then, you had the feeling your mouth was full of sugar. This was its only redeeming feature. Never did know if it did any good. Another use for this plant was its use as a soap. The crushed leaves and water would lather up and wash you squeaky clean. So there you have it - Nikau tree bread and water for food and Kumeraho for soap.

Note - I recently spoke with a cousin in New Zealand and asked if he was familiar with the Kumeraho plant? He was but told me that the younger generation was not. He further informed me that the native Maoris would not discuss the weed with the white man *(Pakeha)* anymore. It appears it is now a closely guarded Maori secret. Why?

Sulfur and Treacle was mixed for sores and boils of which we seemed to have a lot of during the colder winter months. Taken internally. Horrible tasting stuff but we had to take or else. We never found out what the 'or else' was. Must have worked for me as I never had boils, although I did suffer from the sores and scrapes young growing boys get.

Boils are a painful infection, sometimes called a Fun-uncle, is caused by infection of the hair follicle. Older people seemed to have boils more than the children. Probably due to a lack of something in the diet, or by chaffing of clothing. Boils were a common occurrence back then. I remember that the core of some boils were sometimes removed by putting hot water in a bottle to heat it, the hot water was then poured out and the bottle neck was placed over the boil core. The vacuum pulled the core out.

Remember there were no doctors handy in those days. The nearest was 15 miles away, and we had no way to get there unless we hired someone with a car in an emergency. I was told the hot bottle treatment was very painful very, but also highly effective.

THE TAX SNOOPER

This actually happened, probably in the mid 1930's

The IRS *(Infernal(?) land Revenue Service)* agent came nosing around checking on the casual labor workers in the farming area we lived in, supposedly to make sure they were being treated fairly by the land owners who hired them.   Times were very hard and work was not plentiful for the transient.   The following interview with Dad supposedly went something like this.

Agent - "Mr. Leaming how many men are working for you?"

Dad - "One."

Agent - "How much does he earn?"

Dad told him.

Agent - "Only one - no one else?"

Dad - "Well - there is the local idiot."

Agent - "Oh, how many hours a week does he work?"

Dad - "From sunrise to sunset with Sundays off."

Agent - "Oh I see, and what does he earn?"

Dad - "Well let's see; his tobacco, his tucker, (food) a place to sleep, and several bob *(shillings)* a week.
(Approximately 50cents in those days)

Upon hearing this, the agent was sure Dad was taking advantage of the poor fellow.

Agent -   "I want to meet and speak with this man."
Dad -   "Meet him hell - you have - you are talking to him."

Times were very hard back then and Dad sometimes helped others by offering a transient worker a few days work, often going without himself.

The lesson here was that others are important too and are entitled to earn a living if they so desire.

WATCH THE LIONS FEED

On the rare occasion that we had a visitor during meal time Dad would always invite the visitor in using the above remark, followed by an invitation to join us for the meal. He would say "Come on in and watch the lions feed", followed by "pull up a chair and join us."

Dad was always a very hospitable host even if the visitor had wronged him in the past. That did not matter. Meal-time was not the time for quarrels.
He never let meal-times become a time to discuss business matters or become a griping session from anyone. He enjoyed family time at the table, and as a result so did the rest of the family. As children we only spoke when spoken to, or to ask for something. The adults spoke but little also, but when they did, we, as children, were not to interrupt with questions or comments. We were to listen and learn.

The lesson learned here was that there is a time and place for everything.

JIMMY O'GOBLINS

This most unusual term was used by Dad, indicating the amount money any specific item cost, especially if the amount was, in his opinion, higher that it should reasonably be.

For example, if someone asked Dad the price of something, and he thought it was overpriced, he would quote an amount in so many Jimmy o'goblins. As a young man I used to chuckle whenever he used this term. However the meaning and the lessons were clear.

Never be afraid to question anything, if in doubt.

SHARP TOOLS & STRONG MEN

Only on very difficult jobs, where the manpower was not what it should have been, but the final result was accomplished correctly to the satisfaction all concerned, did my Dad comment,

"The tools were sharp and the men were strong."

This comment often gave me, as a young man, great satisfaction especially, if I was one of the participants in the project.   Praise is always welcome especially if it is for a job well done.

WHAT IS FACT?

If something was not quite clearly expressed and fully explained so that Dad fully understood it and he questioned its veracity, after someone said, "Arthur that is a fact", then Dad would say, "Well now you know what fact is? - it's a lie and a half."   This usually prompted chuckles from those explaining.

The ice would be broken and the discussion would continue. Secretly I felt that he was often convinced but wanted to be absolutely sure, hence the quote.

I learned to never take anything at face value.

MARRIAGE & MONEY

As I was growing into manhood Dad and I often spoke about my future. We spoke about many things my including life's work, marriage, honesty always being the policy, and how to treat others especially those less fortunate than us. The latter was hard for me to conceive as we were so poor that even the mice shared their cheese, if they had any. However those around us were not much better off than we were, and most families in the area were in the same condition.

The lessons seemed odd at the time to a young man, but I have learned that they were right on the money. Dad was a wiser man than I gave him credit for at the time. I remember often telling him he was an old fuddy-duddy. Then like Mark Twain I was surprised how much Dad had learned when I reached manhood.

Several lessons have stayed with me through the years:

<u>Do not marry for money</u> - however try to fall in love with a female that's loaded. Good advice perhaps which I did not follow much to my delight - I got lucky and found just the right lady who would put up with my cantankerous ways.

The second lesson was given from a farmer's point of view regarding the breeding of healthy, sound stock. "<u>Try and find a mate with good broad hips</u> who will give you good healthy children." Advice heeded.

A PENNY HORRIBLE

During the late 1800s and the earl part of the 1900s there were many short stories in print in small easy to read booklets which cost a penny or two.

There were for instance stories of the American wild west; stories of wars, stories of romance, etc. My Dad referred to these so called literary works as "Penny Horribles." When ever I see short romance stories about the house *(My wife reads them)* I refer to them the same way, much to my wife's annoyance.

HOSPITAL MOTION

Dad was a staunch supporter of the Labor Party and ran for parliament on several occasions always being beaten by the National Party incumbent. A lifelong friend of his, Arthur Fennell and Dad had many a session together regarding the affairs of the country and the way things were being run. A humorous story Dad told on many occasions was as follows.

The incumbent prime minister was hospitalized and needed a bed pan. There were several of the prime minister's supporters in the outer ward, also hospitalized. As the nurse in training, bearing the bed pan and contents walked through the ward the prime minister's supporters said loudly as she passed each one - "Aye." Naturally the young nurse was embarrassed and she complained to the ward supervisor who then asked the offending patients.

"Well", said one of them, *"This is the first time the premier has made a motion that was carried unanimously without any opposition."*

ANOTHER CRIPPLE

During my younger years I had a grand-uncle who was an unmitigated liar and had the foulest mouth of anyone I have ever heard, even to this day. His language was so foul that many womenfolk would not allow him in their house for a meal during harvest time but took his plate out to him. However, he loved to hunt and fish. He once told me the following story:

"I was hunting and I saw two rabbits several feet apart. I fired at the first one and when I thought half of the shot had left the barrel I switched the aim to the second rabbit and killed them both."

He often came in from hunting empty handed and when he was asked why he would say, "Well, I had several shots and hit several rabbits but they got away." To which anyone listening would exclaim loudly, Another cripple.

This comment became the watchword cry of mine and my Dad's whenever I shot at something and missed.

Years later I read a story about a hunter who was out hunting with an old muzzle loader rifle. He was ramming home the ball when he spied a rabbit across the creek. Without thinking he raised the rifle and fired. His shot killed the rabbit and the ramrod fell into the creek and speared a large fish.

The recoil knocked him over and he fell onto another rabbit and killed it also. His foot kicked a nearby bank unearthing a bee-hive from which he got a bucket of honey. Perhaps this story would top my uncle's.

At an early age I learned that foul talk does not make the man.

STEP-MOTHER FIRST

At meal times Dad always carved the meat and cut the bread. He always served his wife first calling her

"Girl." It did not matter who was visiting, she was always first. Over the years many folk noticed this and some even commented about it.

He said it was his way of saying that she was first, and best thing in his life. And she was too, even though my life, and that of my sister Delphine, was not always a bed of roses. Step-mother always favored her own two daughters ahead of us.

The lesson here is that others should always be considered.

MICK OR MACK

To put this remark into focus for the reader, it must be understood that the Catholic Church was not held in high esteem by the general populace at large in New Zealand at this time. There were only several Catholic families in our area. While these families were treated with due deference by their neighbors, they were not popular and others did not readily associate with them. A "shunning" sort of.

There was no Catholic Church in the immediate are, the nearest being some fifteen miles distant and not well attended. Also, the power of the Catholic Church had just been reinstated by Mussolini in 1929. The Pope had received the keys to the Vatican and now the church was flexing its muscle somewhat.
However quite possibly the main hang-up was the fact that if a protestant married a catholic, the children, if any, would have to raised in the catholic faith, and this had to be sworn to in writing, a practice that has not changed to this day.

Another was the fact, that young women were encouraged to become nuns. And still another was that Dad's youngest sister Marjorie converted to Catholicism. He was devastated.

This is how it was - the background of the time. Since many Irish names started with Mc it was to be assumed, correctly or not, that they were Irish, and as Ireland was a Catholic country, then they would most probably be of the Catholic faith.

Following this same line of reasoning and since many Scottish names started with Mac, and as Scotland was a Protestant country, it could therefore be reasonably assumed that anyone with name starting with Mac would probably be a Protestant.

As a result when someone introduced himself as Mc or Mac *(they sound alike)* the person might be asked, "Is that Mick or Mack. By asking this question the asking party would know *(not always a true barometer)* if the person was a Catholic or Protestant and would treat them accordingly.

While this sounds out of place in today's society, and I wonder if it is, we must remember the times. A common derogatory remark that reflected the way people felt about the Catholic religion, and the Irish who were mostly of that faith, was to call a man "A dirty Mick." The derogatory slur "Dirty Mick" is/was still used in the US and in particular the New York City area. This real slur was usually an invitation to fight. This is probably why it took the Irish such a long time to be considered equals with the rest of society. The lesson here is that time is a great healer and that all men are equal before God and should be trated accordingly.

THE KING AND THE POPE

In the same vein, my step-sister was getting married, but for Dad there was a problem - she was marrying a very devout Catholic. For Dad this was a serious problem. The wedding was to be several hundred miles from our home. Dad and my step-mother were invited and attended. I was not invited as I was not on good terms with the groom who was, in my opinion, an arrogant stuffed-shirt individual. Remember I was young, self assured and not at all dogmatic - I said what I felt regardless of the consequences. I still do.

The wedding proceeded on schedule and the time for the toasts arrived. To start the proceedings the first toast was offered, *"To the Pope and the King."* As my Dad told it, he had his glass half way up when he stopped and remarked,

"No way, no one comes ahead of my King", he said, - *"To the King and the Pope."*

Dad was a loyal royalist and believed that the monarch, his King, was the real head of state.

He later remarked that several people gave him very odd looks. To give Dad his due it took a lot of guts to do that in a catholic gathering. There is a good lesson here - tolerance of others and their views should always be considered.

DON'T WASTE A GRAVE

The tall stately New Zealand Kauri tree *(Native name "Te Tanu" - God of the forest)* has as its sap a gum-like substance that becomes hard and clear when dry. It was used for glues, perfumes and other items. As the trees died, were destroyed or were damaged, sometimes by fire, the gum solidified in the ground and was later prospected for and dug up by the early settlers in New Zealand.

As the prospectors went about and dug the gum, they left many holes, some quite deep, usually left open and uncovered. As a result there were many holes scattered about. Dad often joked, that rather than take up land space with a grave, it would be better to place him in a gum hole, cover him up and plant pumpkins on top as he would be good fertilizer. It did not happen. He is buried beside his second wife in New Zealand, in the Wainui community cemetery, the area where he lived most of his adult life.

THE PICK HANDLE

When Dad was in his 50's, he used to jokingly remark, that a man's usefulness was over when he reached 60 years of age. Back in those days the hard work and the heavy meat diet without proper nutrition as we now know it today, coupled with long hours of hard work took its toll on those who worked the land. It was a really hard life.

In-spite-of Dad's joke to be laid out with a pick-handle, when he was 60, he relented when the time arrived. Several members of parliament with whom he had joked, reminded him about what he had said, and he remarked that perhaps he would enjoy a little more time.

He lived to be 66, spending the last six months of his life with us. He died at sea on his way home to New Zealand after visiting us in the States.

A WORK DAY

Dad and I were up at 4am every day, rain, hail, cold or fair weather, even when he was so sick he could hardly move. He milked the herd, cleaned up and was at the house for breakfast at about 8am. Then the day's work started in earnest. Fences to mend, hay to be put up, cattle to tend, timber to cut and mill, along with dozens of other chores that make a farm run efficiently. Then at 4.30 pm there were the cows to milk again and be put away, and the cleanup.

The evening meal was about 7pm followed by bed at 8pm. Of course I was a helper too. Six to seven hours sleep was all we ever got.

I learned early in life that work is a big part of living and if one wants to eat one must work. It is a pity, that today, many of the younger folk have never learned this lesson.

DAD AND POEMS

Community gatherings *(called smoke-O's or smoke concerts, due to the smoke-fog from those who smoked)* were fairly common, and those present sometimes rendered a song, story or recital. Here is a short poem that was, over the years, recited by several family members as I was becoming a young man heading toward adulthood. The poem must be at least 85 years old, perhaps much older, and it was a particular favorite of my father, and also of mine. Dad recited it often.

Dad's comment was, *"It is always correct to say something nice to people, especially to those who wait upon you, or serve you in some capacity. Remember, that these folk put in a hard day, and many people speak unkindly to them, or abuse them in some way, or grumble about what they do. It does no harm to speak a friendly word, or to compliment them. You may be the only person to say a kind word to them that day." Based on this advice I always make it point to thank folks for what they do me. A nice tip, if appropriate, also says "thank you."*

APPROBATION, poem
(The poem's original author is unknown to me.)
If with pleasure you are viewing any work a friend is doing
and you like him or you love him tell him now.
Do not with hold your approbation until the preacher makes oration
and he lies with snowy lilies on his brow.

For no matter how you shout it, he'll not know a thing about   it, He will not know how many teardrops you have shed.
So if you think some praise is due him
Now is the time to slip it to him,
For he cannot read his tombstone when he's dead.

More than fame and more than money is the comment kind and sunny, and the beauty of the warm approval of a friend.
For it gives to life a savor and it makes you stronger, braver and it gives you heart and courage to the end.
If he earns your praise
Bestow it, if you like him let him know it,
Let the words of true encouragement be said.

Do not wait 'til life is over and he sleeps beneath the clover,
For he cannot read his tombstone when he's dead.

BLACK AS A PRIEST'S HEART

This comment came about as result of Dad's dislike for the Roman clergy and the high and mighty, *"We cannot possibly be wrong"* attitude displayed by priests whenever one visited the area to encourage and counsel their faithful.

As I mentioned earlier there was no love lost between them and the community. Sometimes when thunder clouds were rolling in and the sky was dark and black Dad would look up and remark. *"The sky is as black as a priest's heart."*

He often remarked that because of all the stuff that was confessed to the priests they must have hearts as black as coal. I really think the last straw was when one of the prettiest young girls in the area was recruited as a nun and left the neighborhood.

We never saw her again. Dad was quite fond of Alicia as was I, as she was one of my childhood crushes and her twin brothers were my best friends. My father's comments about this episode are not printable. Dad sometimes lacked tolerance.

TABACCO AND WINE

Looking back eighty years or so and reminiscing, it must have been/was hard on Dad, who was a real pioneer in the truest sense of the word. Well or sick, good weather or bad, rain or shine, there was never any time off. The cows had to milked and the animals fed and cared for. The only luxuries Dad allowed himself were his tobacco, an occasional nip of wine, and very occasionally a bottle of beer. He rolled his own cigarettes. The brand name was *"Silver Fern."* His other luxury was a bottle or two of wine bought at Christmas.   I now know how much these little luxuries must have meant to Dad.

For many years a few weeks before Christmas the *"Wine Man",* an elderly chap named Matovitch, *(We called him Old Matty)* called on Dad for a wine tasting, ordering, selling, buying, chin-wagging shooting the breeze session.

He travelled about our area on an old bicycle that had a basket on the handlebars to carry his wine samples and a few personal belongings.   He was always dressed in a nice suit and sported a tie and hat.   He always stayed the night and was off again after breakfast.   He spoke with a very heavy accent I can still hear to this day.   He knew his wines though.

After supper he would produce bottles of various samples for Dad to taste.   Dad would sip one - roll the fluid around in his mouth and offer a comment.   Then the real fun began.

"Try anoother wun Meester Leaming - I tell you true - thiz wun ess a velly goot vine", he would coax.   Or *"See eff you like thiz wun.   It has nece colar and full budy."*

So Dad would try another and another and another, finally getting a little tipsy.   I was allowed to stay up and to witness proceedings, which I considered a real treat.   However, I was never allowed to sample the wares.   *(Sob.)*

Dad would then make his usual Christmas order of six bottles of the vintage he enjoyed the best.   He would say goodnight to the old gent, and we would retire.   The old gent would be gone early the next morning after breakfast, offered by my aunt Nan, who was our house-keeper. They would not see each other again until the next year.

The resultant purchase would be delivered later by mail, always in time for the Christmas holidays, and would last the whole year. Dad was not a drinker, but did enjoy a little wine or a bottle of beer on occasions.

The annual wine buying episode went on until Dad remarried my step-mother, who was a bit if a prude. That ended that - a pity. Perhaps the Bible passage A little wine for the stomach's sake would apply here.

WHAT IS MONEY?

Cash money was something we saw very little of during those lean years but we always had enough to eat. Dad's motto was that money was not everything in life but that it was away out in front of whatever was in second place. I agree - it still is.

MAN, MOSQUITOES, AND A CALF

My dad's best friend Walker Brunton was born and raised a city slicker, and came to our farming area to get away from it all, and to enjoy the fresh country air. At least that was what he told us, but we all wondered f he would stick it out. After all, life on a country dairy farm is not easy. The work was hard and varied; the hours were long and tedious, and the wages low. There were no eight to five days. It was sunup to sundown and beyond, every day.

 Dad sometimes commented that his work day was from son-up to son-down. However, Walker surprised us all, in that he was eager to learn, worked hard and long, and he acquitted himself well with Dad and all the neighbors he worked for.

He was in his mid-twenties, single, witty, with a quick ready smile. Not surprisingly quite a few of the young females, including several of the local farmer's wives, succumbed to his quick wit and ready charm. If any of the men-folk knew what was going on they wisely kept their own counsel. He left behind one known daughter. The wife's husband never knew, but the entire neighborhood did. Walker was popular and loved every minute of it. He was in heaven.

He had however one glaring fault; nothing was impossible; he would tackle anything - he feared neither man, nor beast and this last was to be his undoing. He had chased and outran a wayward calf for over a mile before catching it.He then carried it back on his shoulders in order to win a small bet of one shilling. *(About 25c)*

He loudly boasted to Dad that he could outfox even the mosquitoes. Late in the day the air was literally black with their swarms.

He contended that they never bothered him and was willing to prove it the hard way. He agreed to strip naked, except for his boots, and be tied with hands behind him to a post where the swarms were the thickest.

The bet was he would stay tied there for ten minutes. Now ten minutes is a long time to be feeding hungry man-eating mosquitoes. I have seen some over three quarters of an inch long.

Dad agreed to let him prove himself, the bet was agreed upon, and at dusk when the mosquito swarms were the worst he stripped down, and Dad tied him to a post in the "Calf Pen" near the cowshed. Dad and I then retired to inside the cowshed to be away from this hungry hoard. Four minutes went by; five, six, seven.

My dad finally called out, *"How are you doing out there Walker?"* Walker replied, *"Oh I'm fine Arthur thank you, but would you please come down and take the darn calf away."* We laughed about this episode for years and I still smile when I think about it.

In 1939 Walker Brunton volunteered for Army service in WW 2. Our small farming community held a fare the well dance and party in his honor. I still remember the last words I heard him say.
"I will often think of you all when I am far away."
Sadly, sometime later we were notified later that he had died of wounds suffered in Egypt.

HARVEST FOOD

Food was a very important part of life, especially so, during the harvest season. The farmer's wives were in charge of feeding the workers. Each farmer's wife made meals they were competent with. For lunch Step-mother usually serve her famous lettuce salad and special dressing along with bread, cold meat, and of course hot tea.

For morning and afternoon breaks *(Morning and afternoon tea)* the fare was usually hot scones *(Recipe follows)* and hot tea. The morning and afternoon breaks were short, lunch lasted about 45minutes. As a youngster I learned a lot by just being quiet and listening to the men-folk talk. Farming and current events, were the usual topics. Today's youth would do well to emulate.

As Abraham Lincoln once said, "*It is better to remain silent and be thought a fool, than to speak and remove all doubt.*" Or as John Wayne once remarked, "*Speak soft, speak slow and don't say too much.*"

Sometimes Dad, who admired Abraham Lincoln greatly, quoted what he is supposed to have once remarked. "*You can fool some of the people all of the time, and all of the people some of the time, but you cannot fool all of the people all of the time.*"

OATMEAL AND WATER

One very important lesson learned from Dad was what to drink in the harvest field when hot and thirsty. Ice was not an option; it was not available to cool the water in those days, so an alternative was in common usage by all the farmers. Two to five pounds of oatmeal in a 20 gallon water container, usually a milk can, stirred well before imbibing, was the best drink available as a thirst quencher. You might say it was a chew drink in that some of the swollen oatmeal was in the cup.

Refreshing! Note - Everyone used the same dipper.

NEW ZEALAND "SCONES"

Recipe for Plain, Cheese, or Date.
We still use this recipe to this day.

2 cups of flour
2 tablespoon of baking powder, slightly heaped
1 tablespoon of sugar
1 pinch of salt
2 ounces of margarine
Milk to mix - approximately one cup
1/2 cup of chopped dates or grated cheese.
Method - Sift all the dry ingredients together thoroughly and then rub or cut in with a knife, the margarine. Add enough milk to make soft dough.
Mix quickly and turn out onto a lightly floured board. Press or roll out lightly forming a square about 1" thick.
Cut into squares *(about 2")* and place on a slightly greased tray. Bake in a quick oven at 450 degrees for 10-15 minutes until very slightly brown. For a glaze *(optional)* brush with milk before baking
(Note baking time will depend upon the size of the scones.
When baking is complete remove from the oven and cover with a tea towel for a few minutes. We use a slightly damp towel. *(Note plain scones are great served with strawberry or blackberry jam with a whipped cream topping.)*

Ideas - Use Rice Milk instead of the regular and the results are just as good. Also used raisins or grated cheese instead of dates. This recipe makes about 12 - 2"x 2" scones - we always double the ingredient amount.
Note - Americans call scones biscuits.

HARVEST BEER

The usual hay-making season lasts about a month overall as all the farmers worked together and cut hay at different times so as to be able to help each other. Hay-making is not a one man task. When our turn came to cut and prepare the hay, Dad would hand me a bag *(it clinked)* of quart beer bottles with instructions to take it carefully down to the spring and leave it there to cool in the water until the harvesting was finished. Some other farmers did the same thing - while others put on a nice meal to show their appreciation.

When the last bale was being stacked, Dad would nod to me and I was off like a shot, to carefully retrieve the sack of bottles. The men would sit around, chat, smoke and drink for about fifteen minutes before leaving for their homes.

When I was quite young I was only allowed a mouthful or two from Dad's bottle - however once I became a teenager and could do a man's work I was included as one of the men and given a full bottle. Yeah!

KILL AND BUTCHER

One year when things were very tight financially, Dad traded timber for 30 scrub lambs. They were real awful looking, but at least they were alive. They were runts, the outcasts, those the sheep breeder did not want. Dad turned them out to pasture to run wild. Our farm was 156 acres and had only a fence around the perimeter. The lambs flourished and grew fat. So, later that year Dad killed one a week and we had meat on the table. My job was to round them up and pen them. Dad showed me how to tell the best and fattest for slaughter. He would feel around the tail area and select the fattest one. *(Fat around the tail area denotes the lamb's condition)*

An interesting point here is that a lamb/sheep will not beg for mercy when it knows it is about to die. However a goat will bleat and cry. Once the lamb was killed Dad put it up on a rope strung over the cross-arms of the power pole by the cowshed. The carcass was then skinned, gutted and left overnight to cool. I still remember the process well.

Dad was a good teacher and knew what he was doing. The skin was slit down the middle of the belly. It then came off in one piece to be washed, cleaned, cured and dried, and later used in the home as a nice warm rug. The warm dressed carcass was then hoisted up high, so as to be away from dogs to cool.

Our dog was in dog-heaven, as he was given some of the offal as a treat. The rest was buried. The butchering took place about daybreak the following morning. Breakfast for the next few mornings were treats to be remembered.

Lamb's fry *(liver)* and bacon, loin lamb chops and eggs along with fried potatoes were/are meals I still remember well. The roast lamb dinners that followed, served with mint sauce, potatoes, and green peas etc. were also memorable. Those were the GOOD ole days! We were poor but we ate well.
If a steer had been butchered the meat was preserved in brine consisting of enough salt in a tub of water so that a potato would float.

TWELVE BASKETS FULL

Whenever we went on a picnic or an outdoor event where there was an abundance of good things to eat, Dad often remarked when everyone had finished, - "And they gathered up the fragments thereof, twelve baskets full." *(Matthew 13:37 and Mark 6:43)* His way of saying we were to be thankful for what we had. We may have been poor but we never went hungry, and we were thankful for what we had. We always had a good big garden too.

ROBERT REECE,
One of Dad's favorite poems.

One of the poems Dad recited quite often was what he
called "Robert Reece." Actually it is one of the
humorous poems written by Carolyn Wells
(6/18/1862 - 3/26/1942 aka Roland Wright titled,
"   *An Overworked Elocutionist."*
The date is unknown to me but was probably written
prior to 1930. He taught it to me and I still recite it
myself some 80+ years later.
I have included it because it was/is a part of my Dad
fondly remembered:

There was once a little boy whose name was Robert
Reese,
And every Friday afternoon he had to speak a piece.
So many poems thus he learned,
that soon he had quite a store
Of recitations in his brain
and he still kept learning more.
And so this is what happened!

He was called upon one week,
And totally forgot the piece he was about to speak.
He brain he cudgeled,
not a word remained in his head
And so he spoke at random, and this is what he said!

My beautiful, my beautiful,
who standeth proudly by,
It was the schooner Hesperus and
the breaking waves dashed high.
Why is this forum crowded?
What means this stir in Rome?
Under the spreading chestnut tree,
there is no place like home.

When freedom from her mountain heights
cried twinkle little star
Shoot if you must this old grey head,
King Henry of Navarre.
If you're waking call me early,
to be or not to be,
The curfew must not ring tonight,
oh, woodsman spare that tree.

Charge Chester, Charge, On Stanley, on,
and let who will be clever,
The boy stood on the burning deck,
but I go on forever!

His elocution was superb;
his voice and gestures fine;
His schoolmates all applauded
as he finished the last line.
"I see it doesn't matter," Robert thought,
"what words I say,
So long as I declaim with oratorical display."

FLYING BREAD KNIFE HANDLE

As mentioned earlier, Dad always cut the bread and carved the meat. The serrated bread knife blade was about 10 inches long with a 4 inch round wooden handle. The blade was flexible. Dad used this knife to discipline us about "elbows on the table." He would pick it up by the end of the blade and swat at our elbows with the handle end. He was very quick and often connected until we got the message. Ouch! My sisters and I learned very quickly to watch the hand that handled this dreaded sit-up and keep your elbows off the table, attention getter.

Lesson - table manners are important.

Dad hated noise, especially when trying to read or listening to the radio and the parliamentary debates. If we got a bit obstreperous, he never yelled or raised his voice to quiet us. He just waited until he caught our eye and then the look he gave was all we needed to settle down. It was that "be quiet look or else" look that only fathers and mothers use on siblings.

We always got the message.

SMOKE-O

This was/is a common term used by many, as a signal for a work break. How I looked forward to the time, when after working hard, dripping with sweat and running out of steam, Dad would say *"Smoke-O"*. I must also point out here that even though I was very young, 7-13, I had to pull my full weight as much as a young boy could. No excuses.

Perhaps the newer younger generations would do well to emulate such work habits. Hard work is a great teacher, and is good for the constitution.

Dad carried the same "West-clock Ben" pocket watch in a small leather pouch on his belt for 17 years. By that time it ran slow about 20 minutes a day so Dad compensated every evening. He finally purchased a new one. However he never really needed a watch as he could look at the sun and tell the time within about 15 minutes. I never could.

When we were working in the bush splitting timber for posts or fence battens, or anywhere on the farm where it was too far to go home for lunch, I would wait for the signal to "Go boil the billy son", which was a 7lb Treacle can with the top removed and a wire handle added. It held about 3 pints.

I would fill the billy at the creek, start a small fire and suspend the full billy on a green stick suspended by two forked sticks. An interesting note here is that I always placed a tiny green twig across the top of the billy.. This prevented the water from becoming smoked and having a smokie taste.

When the water boiled I added the handful of tea and allowed the water to boil for another 15 seconds or so before removing the billy from the flames. The side of the billy was then gently tapped 10 or 15 times to settle the tealeaves to the bottom. Sugar and milk, carried in small bottles were added if required.

PICNICS IN THE BUSH

Lunch in the bush was always a real treat for me, it was a picnic. The fare was rough, but tasty, usually several thick slices of homemade bread with a meat or cheese filler, and sometimes a slab of homemade cake. During WW2 step-mother made a cake called "The coupon-less Cake." It used no eggs and no sugar, both of which were rationed. It was however, a great tasting cake.

For me, I was with the man I admired most in life, and apart from the work involved, was constantly learning how to be a survivalist, how to start fires with wet wood, how to find food in the bush, how to prepare a livable shelter and so on. The lessons were endless and have proven useful over the years. Little things like a wet twig across the top of the billy to stop the water tasting smokey were one.

Always stretch out and rest for 15-20 minutes after eating was another. Dad always did. The lessons were ongoing and have stood me in good stead throughout life.

MOTHER EARTH

Dad was a great believer in maintaining a common touch, and a common feeling with the earth and his surroundings. He hated unnecessary waste of the earth's resources. "We only use the bounty of nature's plenty that we need to, in order to survive," he would say.

Many a dead tree stood on the property that had not been felled. Dad and Theo Codlin, the friend who worked with him, cleared the land, and because there was a bird nest in a tree it was passed by with the thought it would be felled later after the birds had flown, but of course it never was. And so the lone tree stood as a monument to the man who left it there.

In the early years *(1800s-1920)* many giant Kauri trees *(Te-Tanu)* were felled for ship masts and timber. The heads were left to deteriorate. Whenever we found one Dad unearthed the rubbish and leaves etc. and utilized what he could salvaged for timber around the farm. Some were split into fence battens which were in very high demand because of their grain and durability.

It is noteworthy, that these giant Kauri trees are probably related to the American redwood, as they are/were very large at maturity. *(See "Bury me in a gum hole," above)* The largest living Kauri tree I ever saw still stands in Wainui on property owned by the Lloyd family. There is enough timber in that one tree to build seven average sized houses.

It measures about eight feet in diameter and has no branches for about ninety feet. No vines can climb on it as it sheds its bark each year. It towers over the small parcel of bush that surrounds it. Hence the native name of *"God of the forest"* -Te-Tanu.

As a young man I often spread myself out inside a partially burnt out stump of a once giant Kauri, using it as a place to hide, while shooting rabbits. Some of these majestic giants must have been awesome to behold.

LEARNING POEMS

I sometimes thought Dad had a photographic memory as he could read a poem through several times and then recite it verbatim. He would often recite to me while we were at the cowshed milking. His favorite author was Banjo Paterson, an Australian who wrote about the life and times of folk in the Australian outback during the early 20th century. Dad's favorite, and mine was the epic *poem "The Man from Snowy River."*

Others were, "Mulga Bills Bicycle", "Lost", "A Bush Christening", "The man from Ironbark", and "Saltbush Bill's" to mention a few. He later bought several of the volumes and we went over them together and I committed them to memory, and can recite most of them to this day thanks to his patience and careful instruction to detail. I still have the volumes and will pass them on to my daughters.

CLEARING THE LAND
for cattle pasture

When Dad purchased the land, it was from a man who had inherited it from his father who in turn received from his father. Who had received it as a grant from the Crown; from England's Queen Victoria. It was still in its natural state.

First a lot of timber was felled and sold. Then the rest of the bush was dropped where if fell and burned. The trees left with the bird nests did not survive. The carefully tended fire usually raged for several days, and smoldered for quite a few more. When the embers cooled grass seed was sown in the ash. A natural stream ran the full length of the farm and Dad was careful to leave natural bush about seventy-five yards wide on both sides so as to protect the stream and to provide shelter for livestock. The back part of the land was also left for future timber sales.

The following poem was penned by Dad and is included to verify his commitment. I have no way of knowing if it was actually written by him. The poem is entitled *"Are We Faithful Trustees?"* and is on the following page.

ARE WE FAITHFUL TRUSTEES?
As rected by Arthur L. Leaming

I always contemplate the Earth with reverence.
I like the phrase "Mother Earth."
The source of all our sustenance,
The storehouse of all our supplies,
Our raiment, our shelter, the pathway for our feet:

The final resting place of our worn out bodies
I cannot but regard its depletion as vandalism
and sacrifice.

The good Lord gave us but one Earth.
He gave it for the use of all His children for all time.
We are but His trustees in the occupancy and
preservation of the estate for posterity.

If we despoil it, if we fail to maintain it,
If we leave it less fruitful than we receive it,
Then we are unfaithful trustees.

CUTE SAYING
from the poem, "*The wreck of the Hesperus*"

Young children at school learn different things than
they are taught:
The boy stood on the burning deck
his feet were covered in blisters.
The flames came up and burnt his pants,
and he had to wear his sisters.

WAS IT HEAVY SON?

On rare occasions whenever I happened to picked up something hot that would burn my hand, I would of course let it go and it would fall to the ground. Dad's most unnecessary remark would inevitably be, "Was it heavy son"? His way of enquiring if that was why I had dropped it.

He and I always had a laugh afterwards after I had dipped my tortured fingers in water and he checked to see if the burn was bad.

VOT AM I?

Sometimes when Dad was in a playful mood he poked fun at people with large noses. Not that he was bigoted - he wasn't. He felt the people with noses that commanded the most attention were those who lived in Israel. Since some of them who had trouble with the English language, he would imitate, covering his nose with his hand and say, "Now, - vun guess only before you seen mine nose?" It was quite comical and usually got a lot of laughs.

GOD SAID UNTO MOSES, *"Come..."*

I remember well the times Dad would quote some piece of scripture, even if he never seemed to get the quotation quite right. While he did not mock the Bible or those who believed in it, he fully respected those who did. I never heard Dad profane God's name. There were several acquaintances who tried to instruct Dad regarding the scriptures.
Dad would listen; ask questions regarding this person's faith before making a comment.

However, in the last months of his life when he was visiting us in the USA he was very tolerant of our beliefs and often discussed religion with my wife and myself. Dad was of the old school that taught, if a man is a man, will defend his home and family to the death. And he would have too.

The lesson here is that a real man will always defend and fight for those he loves and for the downtrodden

Sometimes, in jest, Dad quoted the phrase about what God supposedly said to Moses and it was as follows. "God said to Moses. *"Come forth, but Moses came fifth because he slipped on a banana skin, and so God disqualified him for life."*

Dad never stopped us children from occasionally attending a service in the small church about a mile away whenever an itinerant preacher was in the area, which was not often.

On these occasions, sadly I do not ever remember the gospel of a risen Savior ever being presented. Fire and brimstone lectures were the main topics in those days. The lesson here was to respect the feelings and beliefs of others, regardless of your own.

KEWPIE DOLL

One of Dad's funny little stories that really made step-mother giggle every time he told it was as follows. *(A kewpie doll was/is a little cellulite doll made before plastic dolls.)*

The little male kewpie doll was driving along and noticed a little female kewpie doll standing by the side of the road. He stopped the car, opened the car door and said, "Det in." She did. He drove along for a while and then turned to her and asked, *"Anything doing."* She shook her head slowly and said, *"No."*

He stopped the car, opened the door and said, *"Det out."*

THE MOVING FINGER WRITES.........

Dad often quoted famous authors and remarks by great men from the past. He was a very prolific reader when he had time to indulge. This reading trait has been passed down to me, to my elder daughter and to several of my grandchildren also. We all like a good yarn *(story)* as Dad called it.
He introduced me the writings of Zane Grey, H. Rider Haggard, R. M. Ballentyne, Edgar Rice Burrows, Jack London, Daniel Defoe, James Oliver Curwood and many others. How I thrilled to the adventure written by these authors. Dad had read them all and could and did discuss the contents even naming the hero's and the deeds they performed.

Dad often told me that I could travel anywhere, be anyone, and do anything simply by reading a good book. So I did, and in the process learned many important lessons for my later life. When my two daughters were growing up I often read to them adventure stories of wild animals and their adventures. I used to read them a chapter per night and often they were left hanging until the next evening.

Of course, I also embellished the story a wee bit and often stopped at the most exciting place, much to their dismay. Sometimes I relented and read the next chapter to stop their *"Daddy Please"* entreaties.

Dad often quoted from the *"Rubaiyat of Omar Khayam"* volume and one verse in particular stands out and has stood the test of time.

> The moving finger writes; and having writ, moves on; nor all your Piety and Wit shall lure it back to cancel half a line; Nor all your tears wash out a Word of it.

The lesson here is that time and deeds cannot be changed no matter what we do; and that <u>those with knowledge have the power</u>.

MORSE-CODE

During the 30s "Morse Code" was still the way the military services and ships at sea communicated, as did the post office for the use of telegrams and cablegrams. Of course, Morse code had been around for many years prior. The code was patented in the United States in 1840 - number 1647 by Samuel Finley Breeze Morse. *(4/27/1791 - 4/2/1872)* The first telegraphic message sent was 5/24/1844.

The first coast to coast message *(USA)* was transmitted in 1861. As I was then considering a career with the New Zealand Post & Telegraph, which used the system, Dad suggested that we learn it together. So, Dad took a piece of charcoal and wrote the alphabet along with the dots and dashes on the inside cowshed wall about my height.

Every so often when he or I was facing away from the wall one of us would say," what is this letter or that number?" The reply would be the correct sequence of dots and dashes, dashes being pronounced dar and dots being pronounced dit.(e.i. -"K" being dar, dit, dah & Peter being - dit dah dah dit, dit, dah, dit, dit dar dit) Later Dad bought me a Morse code key that had a buzzer and we were able to send and read messages sent to each other with the result that in a few weeks we were getting quite good. I was able to send about twice the speed I could read which is understandable when one considers the brain reacts more quickly to the hand than the ear.

I did later join the New Zealand Post & Telegraph and was in training when the messages started to be sent using a machine that typed a thin strip with the message printed on it. *(The forerunner of the teletype and later the FAX)* An old timer told me on the quiet, that the days of telegraphy were numbered and that I should look elsewhere for a career. I did. It should be noted however that Morse code is not obsolete and is still used when telephone lines are not available. Dad's lesson here was - <u>prepare for whatever you undertake</u>. This will give you an advantage over others who have not/did not prepare.

ABSOLUTELY USELES.

Sometimes the words used to describe a certain thing or event can be most descriptive and leave no doubt as to what the speaker actually meant. Many of the words and phrases Dad used were in this category. When describing something that was of no value for anything he would use the term *"As useless as tits on a boar."*   And to my way of thinking I must agree - there is nothing quite so useless.

MONKEY'S BIRTHDAY

This realy cute saying originated somewhere in antiquity and has been passed down from who knows where or when. Dad often used it and I have passed it on to my children and grandchildren.

Simply put, it means that when the sun is shining, and it is raining, it is a *"Monkey's Birthday."* Until recently I had forgotten about it until my grandson reminded me one day when it was happening.

BONSWERE

Dad had a great sense of humor and one of his favorite jokes was about an elevator operator.
(Elevators were not automatic in these times)
He worked where a Frenchman had an office on the 4th floor. When the Frenchman got into the elevator each morning the operator would address him something like this, *"Bonswere Meswur, compree a foggy morning this morning."*

The Frenchman would nod and after he had exited, the operator would turn to anyone else in the elevator and say, *"French you know, I always speak to him in French."*

FIGHTING
If someone tells you "You are illiterate"

Dad's philosophy was this; suppose someone wants to fight you and insults you by calling you a bastard.
(In New Zealand that was real fighting talk.)

So you fight and fight until you are absolutely done in and are laying on the ground unable to move. Your opponent kicks you in the ribs and says, "*Well... you are still a b....*" You can do nothing about it but lay there and take it.

Dad's point; what did the fight accomplish - was it worth it - did it prove anything.

Perhaps the old adage of *"He who fights and runs away will live to fight another day"* is worth something after all.

Some may say there are things and words one must fight for, and this is true, just as we must fight to defend our freedom.   Fighting of any kind makes absolutely no sense, especially war.   War is simply the result of someone wanting what someone else has and is willing to risk someone else's life to get it.

Those in command never actually get involved. They use others to do their dirty work and accomplish their plans. Having said this I will add that using force to defend yourself, a loved, one or someone who is helpless is, in my opinion, completely justified.

A COUNTRY JOB

Whenever Dad had to repair something, which on a farm is quite often, he did so with the premise that looks and finish took a second place to durability, strength and usefulness.   It had to be sturdy, solid, unbreakable and able to be used for the purpose intended.

Beauty of design never mattered. Hence his saying when a repair or project was completed, "It's good enough for a country job."   I must admit that whenever Dad repaired or fixed it always stayed fixed.

A LITTLE WOODEN GOD

Quite often when the weather was hot and the sweat flowed profusely Dad would make the comment, *"I am as dry as a little wooden god."* I think the quote came reading the poem by J. Milton Hayes, actor and poet, *(1884-1940)* titled the "The green eye of the little yellow god."

He often quoted the line, *"And she jestingly told him that nothing else would do but the green eye of the little yellow god."* This quote came often when we, as children, would ask him what he wanted for his birthday or at Christmas time. So here is the poem:

The Green Eye of the Little Yellow god

There's a one-eyed yellow idol
to the north of Khatmandu
There's a little marble cross below the town;
There's a broken-hearted woman tends the grave
of Mad Carew,
And the little Yellow God forever gazes down.

He was known as "Mad Carew"
by the subs at Khatmandu,
He was hotter than they felt inclined to tell;
But for all his foolish pranks,
he was worshipped in the ranks'
And the Colonel's daughter smiled on him as well.

He had loved her all along,
with a passion of the strong,
The fact that she loved him was plain to all.
She was nearly twenty-one and
arrangements had begun
To celebrate her birthday with a ball.

He wrote to ask her what present she would like
from Mad Carew;
They met next day as he dismissed the squad:
And jestingly she told him that nothing else would do

But the green eye of the little yellow god.

On the night before the dance,
Mad Carew seemed in a trance,
And they chafed at him as they puffed at their cigars:
But for once he failed to smile,
and he sat alone awhile,
Then went out into the night beneath the stars.

He returned before the dawn,
with his shirt and tunic torn,
And a gash across his temple dripping red;
He was patched up right away,
and he slept through all the day,
And the Colonel's daughter watched beside his bed.

He woke at last and asked
if they could send his tunic through;
She brought it, and he thanked her with a nod;
He bade her search the pocket saying
"That's from Mad Carew,"
And she found the little green eye of the god.
She upbraided poor Carew in a way that women do,
Though both her eyes were strangely hot and wet;
But she wouldn't take the stone and
Mad Carew was left alone
With the jewel that he'd chanced his life to get.

When the ball was at its height,
on that still and tropic night.
She thought of him and hurried to his room,
As she crossed the barracks square
she could hear the dreamy air
Of a waltz tune softly stealing thro' the gloom.

His door was open wide,
with silver moonlight shinning through;
The place was wet and slipp'ry where she trod;
An ugly knife lay buried in the heart of Mad Carew,
'Twas the "Vengeance of the Little Yellow God."

There's a one-eyed yellow idol
to the north of Khatmandu,
There's a little marble cross below the town;
There's a broken-hearted woman

tends the grave of Mad Carew,
And the Yellow God forever gazes down.

SLASHING THISTLES
(A lesson about time for a 10 year old!)

One morning after breakfast, Dad told me to take my lunch and the mattock (like a pick axe grubber) and go out into the fields and grub gorse, and thistles, (weeds) all day, until afternoon milking time. With my trusty mattock, my tucker bag (food sack) and my best pal, the dog, away I went. I left the house at about 9 a.m.

Well, I worked hard all morning, occasionally looking at the sky like my Dad did to determine the time. I finally decided it was lunch time. After eating, and having a rest to let my tucker settle, I went back at it. I worked all afternoon and was feeling really tired after such a hard days work. I had even raised a good sweat and felt really good about having done so much work all on my own. After checking the sun in the sky I decided it was almost milking time.

I headed home for a quick afternoon snack before going out for the cows. Imagine my consternation when I discovered it was only 11.30 am. How my Dad laughed and laughed. He talked about it for years. The good part was that I was not sent back out by myself. Dad came with me.

JAW HARPS

Another interesting story my Dad told me went something like this: Two men were sitting in a restaurant. They had ordered meat and dumplings.

When one man forked a dumpling into his mouth it was so hot he spat it out onto the plate, picked it up and threw it out the window into the street saying *"what are those things anyway."* A stray dog was passing by, saw the dumpling and snapped it up. It was still hot. He spat it out and fanned his mouth with his paw. Whereupon the second man said, *"I know what they are; they are jaw harps for dogs."*

BOTTOM IN BOTTOM OUT

Did you know that the telephone wires are twisted one quarter turn between poles? That is, wires have four positions from pole to pole. Starting at the top, inside nearest the pole *(top in)* the wire runs to the outside top position on the next pole *(top out);* then to the bottom outside position on the next pole *(bottom out)* and to the bottom inside position on the next pole *(bottom in).*

The apparent reason for this is that somehow it stops electrical interference during transmission of messages. So we have top in, top out, bottom out, and bottom in.

Now consider a cow and the placement of her teats and starting from the cow's head from the side you are looking at and we have the two front teats top out, furthest away, and top in the closest. The same applies to the rear two.
Here is the reason I mention this. If a particular cow (they all had names) had an infected quarter, *(four teats - four quarters)* it was easy to make a note on the cowshed wall for reference and treatment.

Example - you are facing the cow and the infected quarter nearest to you is at the front that would be top in. This was a really good system especially since most cows usually chose the same bale, some even coming in on their own when their particular bale was vacated.

A lesson learned and used from another technology.

WOMEN

Like all men before him the female sex exasperated Dad, sometimes almost to distraction. But in spite of that he was always respectful of the feminine gender and he really loved his girls as he called them of which there were four; his wife, his natural daughter and his two step-daughters.

Sometimes when he was very upset with one of them he would loudly state, *"Women, I cannot live with them and I cannot live without them and, I don't even want to try to."*

He always taught me that regardless of a women's station in life, whether it was high or low, she was always entitled to respect, as she was the vessel God chose to expand man-kind.

SPELLING WORDS
A Rhyme

Our school teacher required us to learn, spell and repeat 10 words several times each week as a homework assignment. For young folk this was a difficult chore. My Dad came to the rescue.

He would take all the words and make some semblance of a rhyming sentence out of them. While the placement of the words may not have made sense, it sure made it easier to be able to repeat them at school.

It did not take long for the teacher to realize what I was doing and as a result these memory sessions were discontinued. However, the memory lesson learned has helped me throughout life.

TWENTY POUND NOTE
(About $40 at this time)

As I grew up Dad was constantly trying to instill what society considers "The Great Moral Values" I would need as I matured and as life progressed. Accordingly, he taught me a very valuable lesson when I finally left home for good and went out on my own into the world to slay the dragons.

As I was leaving, he pressed a twenty pound note (*about $40 dollars then*) into my hand saying, *"this will tide you over until you get settled. You know you are always welcome to come home for a visit. When you come do come back, bring me the twenty pounds."*

At first, I felt a bit hurt that he would want the money back. Then I realized that it was not the money that really mattered but rather the principle of self-sufficiency. And so, several months later when I returned home for a visit, I brought and presented the twenty. Dad took it too. Another lesson well learned and stored for further use.

SYMPATHY – Non-existent

As I have passed through life I have discovered that mankind on the whole is a race that cares little for his fellow man. Of course, there are notable exceptions, one being the camaraderie I experienced during my military career under fire. Another may be the empathy of pastors toward their parishioners. But for the most part I believe that the adage of *"I'm OK and to heck with you"* is paramount in man's thinking. I learned this lesson very early in life, an occurrence that brought the message home with a terrible jolt. This is a <u>lesson that I have never forgotten</u>.

On day while the men were working at the neighbor's sawmill, Dad fell the ground moaning and clutching his stomach. The neighbor's son, Mervyn, walked by, looked down and said, *"what's the matter Arthur, having a baby."*

I was panicky-stricken. Even as a young lad, I wanted to hit this unfeeling goon for being so callus and unfeeling. However, he was a fully grown man and I was but a boy. Several others, more sympathetic, came to Dad's aid and he was taken to the local doctor and had his appendix removed. I ran the farm for a few days while Dad recovered. The unfeeling neighbor's son was later killed when a tree fell on him. I did not mourn even though his younger brother was one of my best friends.

KNOWLEDGE

As I have travelled through life I have always remembered that those with the know-how seemed to be those who did well and got ahead. At a very early age, and ongoing, Dad insisted *that "Knowledge is Power."* Read, study, and listen to others was what he continually preached. His theory was that those that study situations and learn all they can about any given criteria before acting are those that are usually out in the forefront.

The old adages of *"Look before you leap,"* or *"Open the sack and inspect the contents before you buy,"* would certainly apply.

ROLLS C'NARDLY

Automobiles were new when I was a boy; Model Ts, Essex, Whippet and Reo cars, Diamond T and Vulcan trucks, and many other models were the vehicles of that day. The engines were not too reliable.
The braking system was iffy at best and tires were a joke by today's standards. Roadside repairs were often necessary. As a result the joke-slogan *"Rolls-C'nardley"* was coined. This meant the auto would probably roll down the hills but could hardly get up the other side.

LEAVING THE NEST

When I went away to school in Auckland I attended Seddon Memorial Technical College. I boarded with folks in Herne Bay. I caught the same tramcar, #253, every morning for school and the same one home every night.

I was able, with encouragement by my landlady, Mrs. Anderson, to work on Saturdays doing gardening jobs. Thank goodness Dad had taught me how to work. I earned the magnificent sum of 1/6d (*about a quarter*) an hour, money I saved until I had enough to buy another pair of shoes costing me over 30/- (*About $4.50*).
How proud I was when Dad came to town to see me that I could show him how I had been working and saving, and how wisely I had invested my savings. The *"well done boy"* was music to lighten my heart.

GAS AND A DENTIST

I was 15 years old. My teeth were all pretty bad for some reason and caused me a lot of trouble. The

dentist never asked for my parent's consent.
I suppose he reasoned that my request was enough
He pulled them all, after using gas to put me to sleep.
It was a long time before I could eat a decent meal of
solids.

Since then I have had no tooth aches *(ha ha)* but have
had my share of problems with false ones.

A <u>DANCE AT WAITOKI</u> (Why-toe-key)

The dance was about seven miles away.   Rather than
walk or ride the bike I travelled with a horse and
buggy. It was better than walking, even if I was the
only one there without motorization. Looking back, it
was fun.

<u>WORLD WAR TWO</u>

In 1938 and 1939 dark war clouds gathered and our
country was at war.

News updates were all the more important and as a
young lad I devoured all the war stories of our brave
servicemen.   I chafed at being so young as to not be
able to join up and defend my country.

When I was seventeen and a half Dad allowed me to
join the Royal New Zealand Air Force (*RNZAF*) and
after boot camp in Christchurch I was posted to the
Pacific Theater until hostilities ceased.   I remember
when we heard that the USA had dropped the bomb
on Japan that had ended the war, we turned to each
other asking, **"What on earth is an Atom bomb?"**
We found out later about the horror the people in
Japan must have suffered.   However, it had surely
ended the fighting, so we were grateful. Freedom is

something we must cherish, and if necessary, fight for.

ROYAL NEW ZEALAND AIRFORCE

I was afraid the war *(WW2)* was winding down and I would miss out. In New Zealand it is considered a disgrace to be drafted, and I was anxious to be a part of the war. After much discussion Dad agreed that I could join up. I was 17 ½. After rigorous training at Harewood Air Force Base in southern N.Z. I was finally on my way to do my duty. I was in the service, of the RNZAF.

Just before I left to go overseas with the *(R.N.Z.A.F.)* Royal New Zealand Air Force *(Pacific theater)* in early 1945 I was feted at farewell dance party at the local area hall in Wainui. It was a good affair and all present wished me well and a speedy return home.

The night before I left to go overseas to the Pacific Theater, on my final leave, I was in a pub *(hotel)* in New-market, Auckland, tipping back a few *(sucking up the suds)*, when a police constable came in checking ID's. Twenty-one was the legal age limit in those days and I was only 17. When one of the chaps I was with explained that this was my last night, before shipping out to the Pacific Theater, the constable had a sudden case of eyesight failure when he scrutinized my ID. While he couldn't drink on duty, he was kind enough to buy me one and wish me well. Patriotism was, and still is strong in New Zealand.

Interesting note. Not volunteering for military service was considered very poor form; almost cowardice, in those days. Every young man was expected to do his duty.

MY COMPANION IN THE AIR FORCE
FRANK LLOYD

From the moment I left New Zealand until my return, my constant companion was a man named Frank Lloyd. We were always on the same manifest and appeared to be inseparable as far as postings were concerned. After Espiritu Santu, our first layover was Guadalcanal, the scene of very heavy fighting between American and Japanese forces. The carnage wrought by the fierce battles for supremacy of the island was very evident.

General Tojo's son was reportedly killed and buried on this island which may have accounted for the bitterness of the Japanese defense.

A bit of history *(maybe)*

The following story may, or may not be true.
The Americans claim they buried General Tojo's son on the Island. After putting a hollow steel pipe into his rib cage, they placed earth over the grave. Welded to the top of the pipe was a steel helmet which was to be used as a urinal. This particular desecration was called a 'Gonophone.' Why, I will never know. A sign posted nearby inviting all to participate. I did.

Aside from the regulars assigned, there were hundreds of transients passing through daily to forward assignments. The local climate left very little to be desired, but the lack of working details or training made life thoroughly boring. One thing however, which was interesting, was our study of the locals.

They were short, fuzzy headed totally black, and usually almost naked. They made do with anything our forces discarded. They were totally laid back and really content with life. Frank and I looked forward to being sent on. A week passed, then two, then three. All those we had arrived with had been posted on to various assignments.

Finally, after making many daily complaints, we were sent off to Manus for further assignment, and detailed to join about 30 others to guard the far end of the island. We had nothing to do, but life was wonderful. All we did was eat, sleep, play ping pong or cards, swim, sit around and read or just sit in the sun. Those of us who were scroungers *(most Kiwis are)* fabricated stoves, washing machines and many other little helpful gadgets. Anything to stay busy and occupied.

Once a week we were driven to HQ *(about 20 miles)* for two ice cold cokes and a carton of cigarettes each, plus we were allowed a visit to the tiny PX. Some of us traded the cigarettes for an extra coke or two. Truly, an ice cold coke hits the spot in a hot climate.

Interesting Note -
Beware of getting sunburned. Regulations stated this was a self- inflicted wound. Our medic, a corporal, would open all the sunburn blisters of anyone unlucky enough to get badly burned, with a razor and would then rub in salt to heal the problem. Believe me, after hearing this I was very careful to keep my shirt on.

We were at this location when hostilities ceased and the war was over. None of us at that time knew what an atom bomb was, but we glad the war was over and we could go home.

We were posted to return home to New Zealand and our homeward journey finally found us back at

Espiritu Santu.   Transportation was, for the most part, via Catalina flying boats, although some DC3's were also used.   Everyone was sent home according to their priority status.

After several days, Frank and I, still together, were scheduled for the following day's flight.   Alas, several hours before departure, someone with much more juice than we had, *(and we had none)* bumped us and we were scheduled for the following day.

Later we heard that the plane we were to have been on had just disappeared, never to be heard from again; the theory being that the plane blew up whilst in flight. This will never be known. We did leave the following day. I must say that the flight for a safe trip, was a very prayerful one. Sad to say, over the years I finally lost track of Frank Lloyd. Perhaps we will meet again in the new earth.

HOME FROM WAR

After I was discharged I returned home to a welcome home party, again given in my honor. An illuminated address was presented to me by the residents of the Wainui district. This illuminated address has occupied a place of honor on my living room wall ever since. I occasionally look at it and wonder about the residents that were there. Only about 40 were created. I often wonder how many are left. *(80 years later at this writing)*.

The artist was well known in New Zealand; Henry Lloyd, son in law of the original land owner of the farm that we bought. The best part about these affairs was that all the girls kissed me. The older married ones only hugged me and wished me well. Not they didn't want to kiss me but their husbands were funny about things like that. All the men shook my hand and wished me well. *King for a day.*

AFTER WORLD WAR II WAS OVER

My Uncle Ted *(Edward 1/26/1906 - 2/3/1962)*
Uncle Ted was a butcher. He lived in Papakura, which is almost a suburb of the city of Auckland about 25 miles South. He was also the local bookmaker. He apparently loved the ladies too, as he fathered 10 legitimate children, plus.

Unfortunately, he was also a very heavy drinker, causing his death at the early age of 64. He met my Dad one day after a night of heavy drinking and remarked, "I have just finished 11 double shots, and am just starting to come right." That was well over half a bottle.

His oldest son Keith *(12/2/1929 - 6/28/68)* followed his father's habit of excessive drinking and died when he was 39.

DAD'S FAVORITE SAYINGS

If anyone ever questioned the accuracy of Dad's watch, he would reply saying the following, "The Sun, the Moon and the Stars may be wrong, but my watch is never wrong."

Finally, after many years the watch wore out and started losing time. That ended *the charade.*
Another of Dad's sayings was, "A Women, you can't live with them and you can't live without them; and I don't think I want to try."

If anyone ever visited us while we were eating Dad would say, *"You are just in time to watch the lions feed; sit down and eat with us."* Sometimes the visitor would. Regardless of what visitor had done, or who he/she was, the invitation was always the same.

THE WATERING HOLE

The Patamahoe Pub, near Waiau Pa, was the watering hole for all the local farmers in the area. Saturday was the big day when most of the weekly shopping was done. It was also the place where the local gentry met for a pint or two, to talk about crops, the weather, hay making and etc. I used to patronize this drinking establishment whenever I visited my Uncle Sandy and family after I was grown. There was a sign on the back bar wall which read.

Sunday is our day of rest,
All through the week we do our best,
To fill our glasses to your heart's desire,

We sincerely hope that's all you require.

Local pubs in many areas were, and probably still are, the meeting places for the local residents. A lot of business was transacted over a pint or two of the nasty. It was a place to unwind and relax after the hard toil of working the land and tending the animals. There was nowhere else where men could meet and talk on common ground.

Many farmers went to town every week or two; the town in many instances being only the grocery store, post office, feed store, blacksmith shop and the pub. After all the shopping and trading was over, many stopped in for a quick pint or two while his wife finished shopping at the general store for household items.

The younger generation *(21 years old and over, and you had to be able prove it)* feeling their oats would also hang out and talk about girls, cars, food etc., and I suppose they still do.

Saturday was the big day for these events. Closing time was 6pm. Many workers who got off work at 5pm could make it to the pub for a pint or two before closing. This was commonly known as 'the five o'clock swill.' Today the closing time is much later.

The pubs were closed on Sundays so everyone could attend church. Where I was raised hardly anyone bothered, as the services, if there were any, were very irregular. They were only held if some transient preacher was passing through and felt impressed to preach, which wasn't often.

Any visiting preacher were always housed and fed by someone in the area. The Wainui area boasts a small church that still stands and has been designated a national treasure.   It is maintained by the local residents.

A BUN FIGHT

During this period we often attended dances in the local hall some 3 miles away. Of course, we walked to and from. There were quite a few different dance steps, but the waltz was the most popular.

Jazz, called the one step, which was also in vogue. I I can still see Dad and step-mother walking around the room, he going forward and her backward. It was quite amusing to see. Dad said that while he did not approve of jazz he had better learn it as he figured it was here to stay.

Then there was the supper dance where men asked the lady in his life to dance with him and eat the supper that was then served. This way we all knew who was sweet on whom.

Supper, usually served about 10 p.m., was sandwiches, cake and tea which was provided by the ladies. Sometimes during supper someone would offer a song or a verse of poetry for entertainment. These residential family dance nights were, in the main, the only social life the area residents enjoyed. Many of the locals referred to these dances as, *"The local Bun Fight."*

It was at two of these dances that the locals made me the guest of honor. Once to bid me farewell as I was off to the Pacific Theater during the tail-end of World War Two, and once when I returned home. The second time the local residents presented me with an "Illuminated Address"

A framed statement of good wishes for my service still graces my living room wall. I often look at it, remembering.

The "Illuminated Address" was hand crafted and painted by a well know artist named Lloyd.
It features the logo of the Royal New Zealand Air Force (*RNZAF*) and the lettering is written in "Old English" styling. It read.

The residents of the Wainui District in extending
to Aircraftsman Peter Leaming
Who answered the call of King and Country
in defense of his Homeland
congratulate him on his
Meritorious service Overseas
with the R. N. Z. A. F. in World War II.

We hope that this Address will in future
years remind him of the
esteem and appreciation
in which he is held by the Residents.

We appreciate very much his efforts
Towards an early peace
and trust that his future residence
amongst us will be accompanied by
health happiness and prosperity.

From the Members of the Wainui
Welcome Home Committee.
Chairman. *H. I. Brock*
Secretary *D. Carter.*

EDISON'S PHONOGRAPH

It seems like such a long time ago that I saw and heard my first phonograph. I can still see it to this day out under an apple tree in the yard with the large sound horn hanging from a tree branch. The records were round cylinders and played for only a few minutes. The player had to be wound up after each playing. To me this was a really marvelous machine. Later in my younger years I owned one of the "Edison" machines and with a dozen records.
Alas, I know not where it went.

The evolution of the recording machines is nothing short of amazing. First the round cylinder Edison records, followed by the flat 78rpm, then the 45rpm, then the 33 1/3, 10" discs, and 12" discs, followed by VHF tape, cassette tapes, CD's.
Who knows what will be next?

DAD & HISTORY

Dad was born on November 27, 1900 and so much of what had happened in the late 1800s was recent history to him. Remember, there was no radio or television to keep everyone updated with the latest news. News came via ships from other countries or overland via the horse and rider, or by train. Newspapers printed the news for a wider distribution. Radio was on the horizon.

Often while we all sitting around the fireplace of an evening Dad would relate stories about world events. He often told us about the first flight over the English Channel which took about 12 minutes.

The first flight by a male was by Louis Beriot on July 25,1908 and the first flight by a female was by Harriet Quimby on April 16, 1912.

The distance was 60 miles. She stated her speed was 60 mph; she got lost and landed on a beach where she was welcomed by the local fisher-folk. Today the flight takes only seconds.

He told us about the massacre in the black hole of Calcutta, India (Jun3 20, 1756) where 146 prisoners were crowded overnight into a room measuring only 14' by 18' and 123 suffocated.

He told us about the new invention of the radio for the common folk *(up to this time all we had was a crystal set and earphones)* and the new means of transport, the automobile.

Ford, Reo, Essex, Whippet, Chevrolet, Austin, Rolls-Royce were some of the makes we discussed. Our first car was a twin-ignition 1935 Nash that Dad bought in 1942.

Our first radio, a *"Golden Knight"* was purchased from the Farmers Trading Company in 1933 and was supposedly equipped to receive television, which no doubt was only a selling gimmick, but it worked. *(Yes, salesmen used phony sales pitches way back then)* The radio opened up a whole new world for those of us in the community. The nightly news was listened to with anticipation and great interest. There were also radio programs to entertain, musical interludes and the discussions and speeches broadcast from Parliament House in Wellington, the countries capital. I was allowed to listen to several serial stories and was intrigued at the way I was able let my imagination relate to the hero's portrayals.

Looking back to those times I feel a certain sense of nostalgia; while times were hard and folding money was scarce.

However, we had something that most families do not have today, and that is family cohesion. Also, we never wanted for food and a warm place to rest.
Even to this day we as a family still have a tight knit group, and we, the old folks, are thankful and most grateful that our children and grandchildren still visit us whenever they can.

NEW ZEALAND BIRDS

Pueko Harrier *(hawk)*
Tui (Parson bird) a solid black bird with a tuft of white under its throat
Bellbird (because of the bell like song). Now extinct.
Kakapo
Fantails, (so called because of the fanlike tail).
Native Pigeons. A favorite food of the ancient Maori.
More-pork (Night owl - sounds like he's saying more pork).
Kingfisher, aptly named
Kaka (Parrot)
Rifleman. (N.Z.'s smallest bird)
Tomtit
Parakeet
Robin
Pukekhoes,
Magpie. (*They can imitate almost anything including a squeaking gate)*
Yellow-head, Black-fronted turn, Black-backed gull,
Duck (black teal)
I have never seen a live a *Kiwi, Takahe, Chested Penguin, Bandied dotterel, Royal Albatross*

The New Zealand monetary system
as I was growing up.
(Now on the metric system)

The currency was:

Pounds *(L),*
Shillings *(S)*
Pence *(d)*

commonly called LSD *(this was before drugs)*

240 pence (d) to the pound (L),
12 pence (d) to the shilling (S),
20 shillings (S) to the pound (L)

The currency consisted of the following.

- ½d, <u>*Half-penny*</u> *(Ha-penny),* half of a penny. A copper coin.
- 1d, <u>*Penny*</u> *(*a Copper) A copper coin.
- 3d <u>*Three-pence*</u> (Thripence) A tray bit, so called because it was the smallest silver coin one could put into the church offering plate without looking too cheap.
- 6d <u>*Sixpence*</u> (a Zack), I never found out why it was called that. A silver coin.
- 1/- <u>*Shilling*</u> *(*12d (a bob, a Denar) A Silver coin.
- 2/-<u>*Two shillings*</u> *(*24d, two bob a florin) A Silver coin.
- 2/6 <u>*Two shillings & sixpence*</u> *(*30d, half crown, half dollar, half a case) A Silver coin.
- 5/-,<u>*Five shillings*</u> *(*60d one crown, a case) A Silver coin.

Note - Crowns were not in general circulation however but were issued for special occasions.

- 10/- Note. ½ of a pound, 10 bob a double case.
- L1, Note. One pound, 20/-, 240 pennies. *Commonly referred to as a Quid.*
- L5 Note. Five pounds, *(Five quid.)*
- L10, Note. Ten pounds, *(Ten quid.)*
- L20 Note. Twenty pounds, *(Twenty quid.)*

Trees native to New Zealand.

The New Zealand Plant Conservation Network has published a list of indigenous vascular plants. The list identifies the 574 native trees and shrubs which are endemic to N.Z. and threatened with extinction.

A partial list of the more common varieties used for buildings, furniture, and other various purposes in the area where I was raised.

Rimu *(Red pine)* Used mostly for fine furniture.

Kauri Used for furniture and butter boxes.

Miro Very rare

Matai *(Black pine),*

Kahikatea. *(White pine)* Used for furniture and fence battens.

Totara. *(One of five varieties)* A soft red colored wood used in the production of furniture

Tanekaha Used by farmer as fence battens. Also used for furniture.

Silver pine

Maire

Puriri Mainly used for fence posts and firewood.

Rewarewa Used by farmers for fence battens

Northern Rata Used for firewood and furniture.

Tawhai. *(Celery pine)*

Pukatea

Towhai

Mangeoa

Kaikatea

Toatoa

Hinau N.Z. honeysuckle

Kohikohi

Tawa

Kohekohe

Manuka *(Tea tree)*

Black Matipo

Lacebark *(Six varieties)*

Karaka

Titoki

Cabbage Tree *(Five varieties)*

And non-native Macrocarper, *(Also known Monterey Cypress)* and other imported Pine.

Native flowers and grasses, and other beautiful things.

Kowhai. Of all the beauties in New Zealand none can compare with Kowhai, a yellow honeysuckle like flower (unofficial national emblem),

Pohutukawa's *(Two varieties)* crimson blaze is found along the northern seacoasts, in full bloom for the Christmas season.

Orchids of various kinds which grew wild in the deep bush.

Manuka. Probably the best known tree in New Zealand where I grew up was the Tea Tree. So called because the tree's leaves looked like tea leaves and I understand some of the early settles actually used the leaves for a tea like drink. *(Not for me - it was very bitter)* Manuka is great firewood and was very much in demand by the city dwellers. We cut and sold a lot over the years. A good cash crop.

There are two varieties; the white and the red, with red being the most prolific. The tiny little red or white flowers are about on inch across (like a small daisy) and the center of the flower turns into the seed pod about one half to three quarters across. The leaves and twigs from the top of the tree were used as fire starters in our home and cowshed.

It was my job to gather enough fire starter bundles every Saturday to last the week, a job I detested. However, it was a job that I had to do, *'or else,'* and I did not want to find out what the 'or else' was.

Red and White Rata, a close relation to the Pohutukawa, *(white and red)* starts as a vine which eventually chokes it's host and grows together into a solid tree. Giant Rata trees are always hollow.

Clematis *(Puawananga)* grows throughout the country.

Kaka Beak *(Kowhai-ngutu-kaka)*, a red flower a lot like Kowhai's, grows on a small shrub.

Lancebark flowers in the autumn, a white flower a lot like an American dogwood.

Puriri, flowers a lot like a snap dragon, produce round red berries which the native birds love.

Karaka, berries, which were food for the natives and when fully ripe taste lightly of turpentine.

Toetoe, *(toe-ee toe-ee)* has graceful golden plumes a lot like American pampas grass, and grows along sea coast, coastal swamps and river flats.

Ponga Silvdr Fern *(Bunga - bastardized by the Pakeha.*

One of eight of New Zealand's native ferns. A graceful tree with a porous black outer trunk and large fernlike fronds that waved gracefully in the breeze like the hands of Hawaiian hula dancer. The flowers are curved like a question mark which become new fronds. The interior of the trunk is prized for the beautiful vases etc. that are made from it.

Cutty Grass. I never knew the native name for this grass that grew somewhat like American pampas grass. So called because of the razor sharp edges of the leaves. Most of us experienced the feel of it at least once before we learned.

Wait a Minute - Bush Lawyer. A prickly little vine that clung to clothes with tiny barbs like little fishhooks. We called it wait a minute because you had to wait a minute get it off you. Also called bush lawyer because once it got a hold of you it didn't want let go. *(I didn't make it up - honest.)*

Supple-Jack. A long thin vine which climbs on other trees. So called because it is very supple. We used short pieces as switches to train animals.

LOOKING BACK over the sands of time.

The old adage that *"time waits for no man"* is a reminder that as we age time changes; sometimes for the better and at other times for the not so good. I have lived what some consider a long life of 91+ years and have been privy to many changes and wonderfully amazing things.

Consider what has happened since I was born:

The world population reached 2 billion in 1927 and in 2019 it will reach 7 ½ + billion)

- ❖ Through the presidencies of 15 presidents;
  Calvin Coolidge, *Herbert Hoover*, FDR, *Harry Truman,* Dwight Eisenhower, *JFK,* Lyndon Johnson, *Richard Nixon,* Gerald Ford, *Jimmy Carter*, Ronald Reagan, *H.W. Bush,* Bill Clinton, *G.W. Bush*, B Obama, *Donald Trump.*
  During the reign of 4 English Monarchs;
    George V, *George VI*, Edward VIII, and *Elizabeth II.*
- ❖ During World War II and the bombing of Pearl Harbor. Wyatt Erp was living. (He died in 1929)
- ❖ Mussolini restored the Vatican to the Catholic Church in 1929.
- ❖ Bi-planes were common *(Monoplanes were becoming prevalent)*. Jet planes were invented shortly thereafter by the German Nazi regime.
- ❖ Seaplanes were used as passenger transports *(Called flying boats)*
- ❖ Aircraft carriers were in their infancy
- ❖ Before "Sputnik"
- ❖ Before Men had not landed on the Moon
- ❖ Atomic weapons were not yet invented; nor were atomic submarines or atomic power plants.
- ❖ Before nuclear-powered submarines and ships
- ❖ The *"Atom Bomb"* was used to defeat Japan
- ❖ Electricity was a novelty in many rural areas
- ❖ Automobiles were starting to become the new way to travel
- ❖ Photography was in its infancy as were the telephone and the radio.
- ❖ Before Television was invented but was on the drawing board.
- ❖ And many other wonders; too many to mention…

Finally, after being well instructed and thoroughly indoctrinated in the mysteries and intricacies of life by my Dad, and taught what is required and expected of a man, I left home to be on my own.

The lessons Dad taught have stood me in good stead.

Of course, I have sometimes made mistakes and have been off the track on occasions but always the voice of Dad and his teachings come ringing down through time; just as if they were the words of Jesus.

"This is the way, walk ye in it."

Parents are a wonderful gift given to us by God to show us the way.

We are admonished to honor our parents and to give them due deference. We should.

And I say to my children and grandchildren - *"Til the Shout"*

To God be the Glory, and may you walk with Him through to eternity.

WHEN I WAS A BOY!

- ❖ Radio was something new and we had to use our imagination.
- ❖ All the talent must have come from my side of the family.
- ❖ Today children have it pretty easy.
- ❖ I always asked grandma for a big hug.
- ❖ Dad and I had secrets and Dad said don't tell Mother.
- ❖ Dad and I sometimes went fishing.
- ❖ I had to get up out of bed at 4am every morning to get the cows in.
- ❖ I was usually in bed by 8pm
- ❖ There was no TV. There was no twitter.
- ❖ Dad often told me, "You make me very proud," when I did something special.
- ❖ We were told children came via the stork.
- ❖ Folks would say I was growing like a weed.
- ❖ Dad always helped me with my homework.
- ❖ There were no computers to use for homework.
- ❖ There were only about 2 billion people in the whole world. Now there are 7+ billion. (March 2018.)
- ❖ There were no Aircraft Carriers.
- ❖ Model T vehicles were plentiful, as were Essex, Reo, Diamond T, and Vulcans. Later the Ford Model A were popular.
- ❖ We never locked our house. Everyone was trustworthy.
- ❖ We only bathed once week, even if we did not need to.
- ❖ There was no refrigeration, there was no electricity. We used mantle lamps and candles.
- ❖ I had to walk or run about three miles to school.
- ❖ I had no shoes or boots until I was in my early teens.
- ❖ I warmed my feet on cold mornings by stepping into warm cow pies.
- ❖ We did not have a car or tractor. Horses were in, and we walked.
- ❖ The phonograph used was the Edison with circular records and a very large trumpet like amplifier.
- ❖ Man had not walked on the moon.
- ❖ We killed our own meat, and grew our own vegetables and fruit.
- ❖ There was no internet.
- ❖ There were no cell phones.
- ❖ We had a telephone on a party line with 14 others.

- ❖ We had no central heat, just a large fireplace in the living room.
- ❖ Children were not allowed to talk unless spoken to. Enforced.
- ❖ Our family always ate together and we children stayed at the table until everyone had finished eating.

NOW I AM A GRANDFATHER
MYSELF AND I SOMETIMES SAY......

- ❖ "I was not asleep, I was just resting my eyes."
- ❖ To the children: "Don't believe everything your Grandmother says."
- ❖ After rousting a bit with the children..."Aw, Grandma we were just having a little bit of fun."
- ❖ Listening to the older songs. "Now that was really music."
- ❖ When the children or grandchildren ask to do something my reply usually is, "If it is OK with your grandma, it is OK with me."
- ❖ When the children or grandchildren tell me they love me, I say, "Grandpa loves you too."
- ❖ When I pick up my grandchildren I say,"My but you are getting heavy."
- ❖ When something unusual happens I might say, "<u>Now when I was a boy</u>...."

Other Books and Articles by the Author.

Col. Pete's Korner
History of the Ellijay Seventh-day Adventist church from 1890-2012
Life Poetically. Three Generations. _(Poems and Essays.)_
Will the Vatican rule the World and the Oath of the Jesuit Order
Is the USA dying? _(Six part series)_
Life on the thin Blue _Line_ _(My police officer's story)_
America Today as I see it. (Eighty part series.)
Son of a Pioneer. _(Autobiography.)_

Arthur L. Leaming *(my Dad)* Age 21 years old

Dad's Wedding Photo 1925

The old School House, built in 1879

Arrangements had been made to remove the original school. Efforts were made by the committee to resite it on the sports area for recreational purposes, but without success. It was transported to the Museum of Transport and Technology in Auckland taking pride of place in the pioneer village there.

Wainu School Photo 1939 Pete & Delphine

A Settler's home – Wainui 1870

SCHOOL COMMITTEE		
	Secretary	
E.Scott	1903	T.B.Lamont
T.B.Lamont	1907	F.G.Kinsey
F.G.Kinsey	1911	J.S.King
J.W.Scott	1914	C.Milligan
W.Taylor	1915	T.B.Lamont
A.Levy	1916	Mrs Parker
W.Taylor	1941	A.L. Leaming
G.E.King	1942	G.Baird
H.A.S.Lloyd	1950	R.McCullum
N.E.Lord	1953	G.Main
B.A. Jordan	1954	R.Dixon
J.Sonerson	1957	D.J.Lomax
W.P.King	1959	L.H. King
C.A.King	1961	A.C.Scott
	1963	D.J.Cocks
	1965	H.G.King
	1967	W.P.King
	1975	N.J.Kimpton
	1977	R.T.Lloyd

THE FIRST PUBLIC BUILDING IN WAINUI

Sister Delphine – age 26

My Wedding Photo – February 5, 1957

Postscript

Many years later, having lived in the United States since 1951, I returned to New Zealand, married a childhood sweetheart in 1957, and moved back to the United States. With a wife of over 62 years, two daughters and five grandchildren and one great grand-daughter, it has been a good, full and meaningful life.

During that time, through my wife's ongoing example, I found my *Lord and Savior Jesus*. As reported in *Proverbs 31:10-31*, a good women *(Help Mate)* really does make a difference. Since then my family and I have walked together with *Him* and are active in our church.

One son in law is a Doctor of Chiropractic here in Blue Ridge GA. and the other is home builder and general contractor in Maryville TN.

Often when I reminisce about the past, and look backwards, I can see and understand *God's* leading, and the path laid out for us by our *Lord* before we are even born. It causes me to wonder why we sometimes doubt *His* leading in our lives.

I also wonder *'What if'* I had followed another course of action, but didn't, and praise *His* Hole Name for the path *He* offered. Unknown, to us, our lives do affect the destiny of others. I thank *God He* knows the end from the beginning.

Looking back 89 + years, they were good times, gentler times and I remember them fondly with some nostalgia. Actually, I have come a full circle.

- I have no Television, and no Radio in my home.
- I only read the local country weekly Newspapers. I have lived a really good life, so far, and have absolutely no complaints.
- I have been blessed with a wonderful marriage partner;
- Two beautiful daughters, both of whom have both married good men.
- I have five wonderful grandchildren, and one great granddaughter.
- Perhaps as my end draws nearer on this sick world, it is fitting.
- Let the world, and those in it, who so desire, roll on without me.
- As for myself and my family,
- We wait upon the Lord.
- *"Til the Shout*

Made in the USA
Columbia, SC
29 September 2020

21439157R00100